_____

Presented to

_____

Presented by

_____

Date

MOMENTS
of PEACE
in the
PRESENCE
of GOD
for
COUPLES

MOMENTS
of PEACE
in the
PRESENCE
of GOD
for
COUPLES

*Reflections on God's Promises
and Purpose for Your Marriage*

BETHANYHOUSE

11 12   4 3 2

Grace and peace be yours in abundance through the knowledge of God and of Jesus our Lord.

2 Peter 1:2 NIV

CONTENTS

Introduction

When two of you get together on anything at all on earth and make a prayer of it, my Father in heaven goes into action.

Matthew 18:20 MSG

∞

On the sixth day of creation, God created both man and woman in his image. The Bible says he then blessed Adam and Eve and gave them dominion over the whole earth. From the very beginning, it was God's intention to rule the world by the power of two—two human souls completely committed to each other and to him.

Living together as a married couple is not always easy, but God promises to bless you as you strive to come as one into his presence. He is eager to give you the wisdom and understanding you need to live together in harmony. As you read these devotions, resolve to keep your hearts open to each other and to God. Day by day you will discover anew God's amazing power of two.

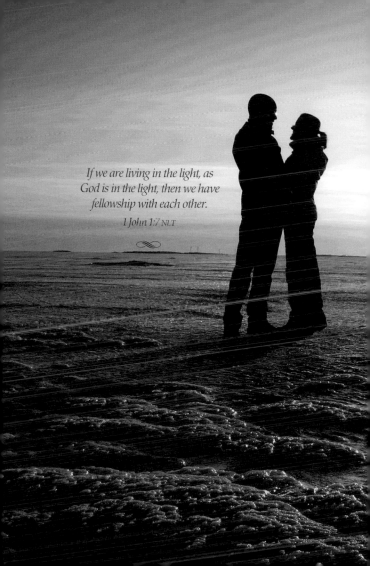

*If we are living in the light, as
God is in the light, then we have
fellowship with each other.*

1 John 1:7 NLT

... you that we ... ...
make it convenient to come in I wonder I am to ...
stopped there I was living as there is another family
... at the house it being very bad and if it ...
... for that I would have written before ... I ...
... before ...

Love

Regardless of what else you put on,
wear love. It's your basic, all-purpose
garment. Never be without it.

Colossians 3:14 MSG

The Way of Love

It is possible to hear the word *love* used in a sacred worship service, a hot dog commercial, a rap tune, and a dozen other places all in the course of one day.

However, the power of love is not negated by its commonness. Love is what brought Jesus from heaven to earth to give himself for us. And love is what he expects us to give him and each other in response to his sacrificial act, love in word and in deed.

Most relationships begin with physical attraction, but that is merely the precursor of real love. Pure and holy love gives all and sees no other. When you take hold of that, nothing can break your bond.

God, we long for a love that is true
and unbreakable. We open our hearts
for you to teach us. Amen.

The whole point of what we're urging is simply love—love uncontaminated by self-interest.

1 Timothy 1:5 MSG

The Power of Love

> *You will keep
> your friends if you
> forgive them.*
> Proverbs 17:9 CEV
> ∾

The first lesson of true love is that it forgives freely. When possible it ignores a wrong done. That concept is simple, yet it is difficult to live with. Human nature seeks validation. It wants the offense acknowledged.

True love sacrifices ego for the sake of the other person and the relationship. It allows you to set yourself aside and lift up another. It takes a negative—a wrong suffered—and transforms it into a positive. It reinforces inside you the nature of the love you have for each other.

Little offenses become big offenses only when they are allowed to smolder. Extinguish them with the water of forgiveness. Let the power of love rule your hearts.

∾

God, help us to overcome the demands of our selfish natures and give ourselves completely to the power of love. Amen.

Love is patient, love is kind. . . .
It keeps no record of wrongs.

1 Corinthians 13:4–5 NIV

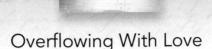

Overflowing With Love

May the Lord make your love increase and overflow for each other and for everyone else.

1 Thessalonians 3:12 NIV

∞

Some people are comfortable with overt expressions of affection. But even if both of you prefer to avoid gushy sentimentality, it's important not to disregard the need for physical and verbal expressions of your feelings for each other.

When served your favorite meal, do you push it around on your plate, taking just an occasional bite? Or do you express your delight by relishing each forkful? Your love for that dish shows on your face, in your demeanor, and usually in your words. In the same way, your physical expressions of love demonstrate to each other and to others that you delight in one another.

Be sure to let your love overflow from your hearts to your affectionate embraces and tender words.

∞

God, help us to see the importance of affirming our love through words and gestures. We thank you for each hug and kiss. Amen.

*Support your faith with . . . endurance,
and endurance with godliness, and
godliness with mutual affection,
and mutual affection with love.*

2 Peter 1:5–7 NRSV

The Last Word

*Christ's love ... has the
first and last word in
everything we do.*
2 Corinthians 5:14 MSG

Marriage isn't easy, but it is worthy of everything you invest in it. It is, in fact, most likely to be the primary tool God uses to teach you to love deeply and truly. He knows that each time the two of you hit a bump in your relationship, you will be challenged to grow in your desire and ability to love.

Agree that when misunderstandings arise, slights happen, and the waters of marital bliss become troubled, you will ask first how Jesus, your example of pure love in action, would respond.

By doing this, you will learn that in marriage, as in every other issue of life, love must have the last word.

Dear God, we want to love as you love. We agree to stop and consider how you would respond to whatever comes our way. Amen.

Love is always supportive, loyal,
hopeful, and trusting.

1 Corinthians 13:7 CEV

Holding On to Love

Most of all, love each other as if your life depended on it. Love makes up for practically anything.

1 Peter 4:8 MSG

Love is an entity with many gradations and degrees. Your love for God and each other must be of the highest order. This means that in the world of human relationships, you must love each other most.

When you married, the vows, the rings, the kiss, and the honeymoon were all intended to enhance and celebrate the loving commitment the two of you alone were making. But in the busyness of everyday life, this is oftentimes lost, pushed aside by a sense of responsibility to work, family, and other concerns.

When you know that each of you comes first with the other, you will be better able to care for your family, jobs, and other pressing issues, and better able to weather any storm.

God, with you as our witness, we renew our commitment to love each other more than we love anyone else in our lives. Amen.

A man shall leave his father and
mother and be joined to his wife,
and they shall become one flesh.
Genesis 2:24 NKJV

Living for Love

Let love be your guide.
Christ loved us and
offered his life for us
as a sacrifice that
pleases God.

Ephesians 5:2 CEV

Some people marry for status, convenience, or money, while others wish to ward off loneliness, insecurity, or unhappiness. Ideally, though, marriage should be the result of a deep love between a man and a woman.

If the two of you married for love, you are most blessed. That love will grace your lives every day and keep your commitment strong regardless of circumstances you might encounter. If you married for any other reason, you too can rejoice, knowing that God is able to give you the love you lack as you live together with your hearts open to him.

Some couples give up too easily. Patience and open hearts will take you places you never expected to be.

God, teach us how to live a life of love every
day as you fill our hearts with more love
than we ever thought possible. Amen.

My lover is mine, and I am his.

Song of Solomon 2:16 NLT

Love in Motion

Let us consider how we may spur one another on toward love and good deeds.

Hebrews 10:24 NIV

When love is idle, it ceases to grow, and when it ceases to grow, it dies. To retain its strength and power in your life, it must always be in motion. It is like your body in this regard. Only when your body is dead does it cease to slough off old cells and create new ones.

For this reason, you cannot depend on memories of love. Each day you must find new reasons to love, new words to communicate it, new ways to affirm it. Love must be fed, watered, and renewed day by day.

Ask God how to keep your love fresh for a lifetime, and he will show you.

God, show us how to keep our love ever in motion, always growing, always surprising us with its brightness. Amen.

*Let us not love in word or in tongue,
but in deed and in truth.*

1 John 3:18 NKJV

The God Kind of Love

I am giving you a new commandment: Love each other. Just as I have loved you, you should love each other.

John 13:34 NLT

∞

In the New Testament, several Greek words refer to love. One of those is *agape*, defined as love that is "charitable, selfless, altruistic, and unconditional." Agape is the kind of love that parents have for their children. Agape is the kind of love that creates goodness in the world. Agape is also the kind of love God is thought to have for humankind, and it is the primary kind of love he wants us to have for each other.

As husband and wife, you will also experience *phileo*, "friendship love," and *eros*, "romantic love." But these should be built on a foundation of agape love. Ask God to show you how to love each other selflessly and unconditionally, just as he loves you both.

∼

God, we want our love to last forever.
Teach us how to love each other
with selfless abandon. Amen.

*Praise the L*ORD *because he is good to us,*
and his love never fails.

1 Chronicles 16:34 CEV

God Is Love

If we love each other, God lives in us, and his love is truly in our hearts.
1 John 4:12 CEV

God is love. That isn't just something we all heard as children. It's truth. Love is the essence of who God is and the motivation for all he does. When God comes to dwell within you through the Holy Spirit, it is as though you have an inner core of love.

That core serves as an unending source of love for God, for each other, and for others. It will serve you as long as you choose to draw from it.

Allow the love of God to overflow within you. It will feel like an alien substance as it encounters your ego and human nature at first. But soon enough, it will permeate everything it touches.

God, we thank you for filling our hearts with your love. Show us how to make that love the defining force within us. Amen.

*God is love, and those who abide in love abide
in God, and God abides in them.*

1 John 4:16 NRSV

The Love Factor

Let no debt remain outstanding, except the continuing debt to love one another.

Romans 13:8 NIV

For believers, the primary goal is to grow into the image of Christ, to be like him in every way possible. Because God is love, being more like him means you become more proficient in the ways of love. You learn to think loving thoughts. You learn to respond with loving words and actions.

Even more wonderful is the thought that as you grow in love, your lives together will also increase in love. Your relationship will grow stronger and stronger. This love factor will sweeten every part of your lives.

Life will never be perfect here on earth. You will still have trials, but you will soon see that love removes the sting.

Dear God, we want to live our lives in love.
Help us to remember that you are love
and that you dwell within us. Amen.

*O God, we meditate on your unfailing love as
we worship in your Temple.*

Psalm 48:9 NLT

Love Is Fearless

There is no room in love for fear. Well-formed love banishes fear.
1 John 4:18 MSG

❧

When two people come together, there is usually a certain degree of fear involved. This might be fear of commitment, fear of abandonment, fear of rejection, fear of failing to meet expectations. The list is quite long and complex.

But the Bible says one of the most amazing aspects of love is that it banishes, vanquishes, overrules, exiles, and kicks fear out of the picture. This is because true love isn't flimsy or superficial. Like the tightrope walker on the wire, it commits completely and works without a net. It is fearless.

Love isn't learned in a day. Start practicing the ways of love, and one day you'll find yourself high in the air sliding effortlessly along the wire.

❧

God, we admit we do have fears. Help us to grow in love until we squeeze those fears out of our lives. Amen.

Don't be afraid, my people. Be glad now and rejoice, for the LORD has done great things.

Joel 2:21 NLT

Loving as Friends

Be sincere in your love for others.
Romans 12:9 CEV
∞

Do the two of you think of each other as good friends? You know—friends are always happy to see each other. When they are together, even hard work seems like fun. They are quick to help each other, even without asking. They are there for each other in the hard times. They confide their secrets and keep their promises. They are loyal, affectionate, and caring.

Friendship is an important element in marriage. It helps to level out the highs and lows of romantic love. And it will help to open up your communication, deepen your trust, and allow your relationship some breathing room.

Look forward to the wonderful blessing of loving each other as friends.

God, help us as we learn to treat each other as friends, having fun together, sharing confidences, keeping promises. Amen.

A friend loves at all times, and kinsfolk are born to share adversity.

Proverbs 17.17 NRSV

Love Is Forever

*Love ... always trusts,
always hopes, and
always endures.
Love never ends.*
1 Corinthians 13:6–8 NCV

When two people commit themselves to each other, typically they begin to invest in life together. They may buy a car, purchase a home, open a savings account, begin a retirement fund, open a stock portfolio, or start a business. These are all great investments, but they are temporary. They last only for a lifetime, if that.

The investment you make in love, however, is an investment that will last forever. Love is the one thing you will take with you when you leave this world.

Spend as much time and effort maintaining your love as you do your bodies, your retirement funds, and your earthly possessions. When other things fail you, love will not.

God, we want to store up treasures in heaven
as well as on earth. Show us how
to increase our love. Amen.

*Stockpile treasure in heaven, where it's safe
from moth and rust and burglars.*

Matthew 6:20 MSG

What Really Matters

The only thing that counts is faith expressing itself through love.

Galatians 5:6 NIV

You may consider yourself a person of faith, conversant in Scripture, committed to God's ways, living a life of personal sacrifice, remembering the poor, moving mountains in prayer, and serving God in every way possible. All these things are pleasing to God. They are the form and substance of his commandments.

But one commandment has precedence over all the others. That is to love. Unless your life of faith is awash in God's love, it is of little consequence. And no matter how good you think your marriage is, it will have no depth unless love rules in your hearts and lives.

Live for love, serve love, and give all you have for love. Without it, nothing really matters.

God, help us as we seek love first.
It is our desire to ensure that our
lives and our faith matter. Amen.

Be kind and bless us!
We depend on you.

Psalm 33:22 cev

The Source of Love

*We love because
he first loved us.*
1 John 4:19 NIV

Some people fall in love at the same moment— two strangers who make an immediate and lasting connection. But in most cases, one person falls in love first and pursues the other.

In our relationship with God, he has always been the pursuer, the one who loved first. Even when humankind turned its back on him, ran away from him, betrayed him, he refused to quit. He set in place his plan to redeem those he loves so much.

God loves you, and he always will. It isn't a trifling thing or something that can be taken for granted. It's serious business, the result of which is that when you turn to him you will find him waiting.

God, you loved us first, before we knew you and even after we turned our backs on you. Teach us how to love you in return. Amen.

The Lord *appeared to us in the past, saying: "I have loved you with an everlasting love; I have drawn you with loving-kindness."*

Jeremiah 31:3 NIV

⚬

The Purity of Love

Love is a hot commodity these days. But what kind of love is it that people are talking about? The popular kind of love is superficial, fickle, and selfish. It wants for itself what the object of its affection brings to the table, whether that is beauty, money, status, or some other prerequisite. It comes and goes with the circumstances.

Real love, pure love, is far less popular than the kind the world dishes out. And it isn't difficult to understand why. The purest love gives without taking, and rather than conquering that other person, it humbly gives itself up, hands itself over.

Look into your hearts. What kind of love are you harboring there?

Dear God, no matter what kind of love
brought us together, we now desire
the purity of true love. Amen.

Set an example for other
followers by what you say
and do, as well as by your
love, faith, and purity.

1 Timothy 4:12 CEV

The Demands of Love

Honor one another
above yourselves.
Romans 12:10 NIV

∽

Some people insist that marriage is a fifty-fifty proposition. This has an appealing and equitable ring to it. But true love is much more exacting. It requires that both partners give 100 percent to the relationship, 100 percent of the time. It's not enough to come halfway. Each person must be willing to give all.

That may sound daunting, but it is, after all, the example that Jesus set. He gave his power, his status, and his earthly life for those he loves, not because it was deserved, but because it was his choice.

Give your all to each other, not because you deserve it, but because it is the secret to a truly worthy love.

∼

God, soften our hearts and make us each
willing to give our all to the other
as we give our all to you. Amen.

Remember this — a farmer who plants only a few
seeds will get a small crop. But the one who
plants generously will get a generous crop.

2 Corinthians 9:6 NLT

The Lessons of Love

You yourselves have been taught by God to love each other.
1 Thessalonians 4:9 NIV

Traditional wisdom says that we "fall" in love. The trouble is that any love we fall *into*, we can easily fall *out of* just as quickly. The true, pure, and lasting God kind of love must be learned.

Fortunately, God is an able teacher. He has already walked the walk and talked the talk. He has already given his all. And he is willing to teach you as you surrender yourselves to him. These lessons come as you experience his pure and lasting love for you and move from insight to insight.

Commit yourselves to learn the lessons of love from the Master Teacher. Love like this will change you both from the inside out.

God, we desire to love truly, to set aside the superficial, and to give ourselves each to the other and each to you in full surrender. Amen.

I will instruct you and teach you in the way you should go; I will guide you with My eye.

Psalm 32:8 NKJV

Unity

❦

Be friendly with everyone.

Romans 12:16 CEV

Living as One

It isn't what you learned in math class, but when it comes to marriage, the Bible says that 1+1=1. Looks somewhat funny, doesn't it? When two people are joined together in marriage, they become one flesh. Notice that they do not become one "person." It isn't as though one of you is integrated into the other and ceases to exist in God's eyes.

God sees the two of you as a single united entity. Think of any business, large or small. Though it's made up of one person or thousands, it presents a united face to the world.

Begin to think of yourselves as one before God. It will change your whole perspective.

God, we thank you for honoring the life we have in common. Help us to better honor it as well, by finding ways to strengthen our unity. Amen.

*I want their hearts to
be encouraged and
united in love.*

Colossians 2:2 NRSV

Bound Together in Peace

*Make every effort to keep
yourselves united in the
Spirit, binding yourselves
together with peace.*

Ephesians 4:3 NLT

∞

God made each of you unique and fully complete. He never expected the two of you to agree on everything. But it is necessary as you face the world together that you agree on some things for the sake of peace. After all, if one of you wants to live in Indiana and the other is set on Georgia, something has to give.

This is an extreme example, but it does illustrate that plenty of issues must be agreed upon. When these things come up, don't try to bully each other or resort to power plays. Instead, ask the Holy Spirit to help you talk out your differences and seek the peace that comes with harmony.

❧

God, we are two very different people with
differing views. Teach us how to walk as one,
so that we might enjoy the blessings and
productivity harmony brings. Amen.

Agree with God, and be at peace;
in this way good will come to you.

Job 22:21 NRSV

Equals in His Eyes

Make me truly happy by agreeing wholeheartedly with each other, loving one another, and working together with one heart and purpose.

Philippians 2:2 NLT

∞

While the Bible tells us that God designed the husband to be the leader in the family, it does not say that the wife is therefore somehow inferior. You were both created in the image of God, fully complete and amazing. There are no inferior people. God's hierarchy is a simple construct to avoid marriages mired in standoffs.

When you see it that way, it's much easier to hear each other and give place to the other in love. The goal is to work together as one, each of you reaching your full potential. What a wonderful life you choose for yourselves when you weave yourselves together to accomplish God's purpose.

∼

God, we lift our faces to you, two people united by love and our commitment to you. Thank you for making us one. Amen.

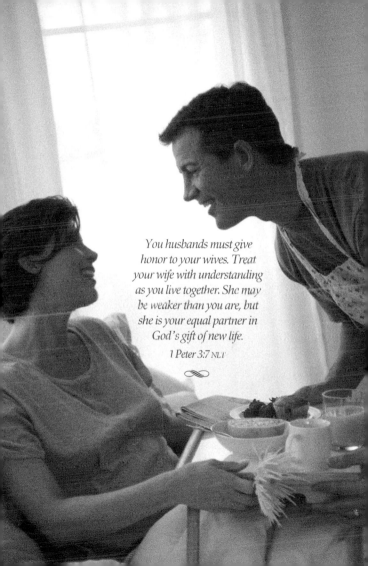

You husbands must give honor to your wives. Treat your wife with understanding as you live together. She may be weaker than you are, but she is your equal partner in God's gift of new life.

1 Peter 3:7 NLT

A Spirit of Unity

*Have unity of spirit,
sympathy, love for one
another, a tender heart,
and a humble mind.*

1 Peter 3:8 NRSV

∞

Living together as one cannot be done in your natural strength. Willpower does not work. It will be possible only when you both submit yourselves to God, when you are willing to lay down your pride and make it a priority to treat each other with tenderness and understanding.

As it does in other aspects of life, the Golden Rule works well here. Treat each other the way you want to be treated. Your egos will balk at the idea, and you will find many excuses for noncompliance. But with God's help, you will get there.

Let the Spirit of unity teach you the benefits and blessings of unity.

∼

God, we submit ourselves to the Spirit of unity,
your Holy Spirit. Show us how to live together
in a way that pleases you. Amen.

This Helper is the Holy Spirit whom the Father will send in my name.

John 14:26 NCV

Committed to Peace

As far as it depends on you, live at peace with everyone.
Romans 12:18 NIV

The Bible's instruction is that you strive to live in harmony with each other, with God's plan, and with others. Don't worry; God knows your differences are great. And still, he urges you to do all you can. That means that the humble mind and tender heart you call to bear on your own marital relationship must also be extended to those outside your marital unit.

Of course, it won't be possible to be in unity with everyone. That's just the way it is. God asks only that you do your part and leave the rest to him. Focus instead on those who have surrendered their lives to the truth of the Bible.

God, it is our desire to live in harmony with those around us. Strike all pride, all prejudice, and unrighteous judgment from our lives. Amen.

*In everything set them an
example by doing what is good.*

Titus 2:7 NIV

Walking Hand in Hand

May the God who gives endurance and encouragement give you a spirit of unity among yourselves as you follow Christ Jesus.

Romans 15:5 NIV

∞

As the dictionary defines *unity*, it is more the ability to live together in peace than to agree on every issue. If you have a disagreement with each other or with someone outside your home, you may work to come to some specific compromise. But living in unity means that you must find ways to get along with others over the long haul. That's a much bigger commitment, one that takes endurance and determination.

When disagreements come—and they will—encourage each other in the lessons of love and the pursuit of peace. Only then will you be able to see beyond your day-to-day differences and walk hand in hand with others.

∽

God, you keep the sun, moon, and stars
moving in harmony with one another and
with your mighty plan. We look to you
to teach us to live in unity. Amen.

Do the hard work of getting along with each other,
treating each other with dignity and honor.

James 3:18 MSG

The Goal of Christ

The goal is for all of them to become one heart and mind—just as you, Father, are in me and I in you, so they might be one heart and mind with us.

John 17:20–21 MSG

Living together in unity can take many forms. Bonnie and Clyde, for example, were certainly united in their quest to rob banks and carry out other criminal pursuits. Your unity cannot be based just on random ideas and opinions. God's call to unity is based on God's opinions and his standard of righteousness.

As you agree, you are not only coming into line with each other but also with God. In many cases, that will mean both of you will have to amend your ways of thinking. In so doing, though, the power of your agreement will be elevated to a place you never thought possible, a place where you are walking in unity with the heart and mind of God.

We thank you, God, for the healthy minds and loving hearts you have given us. Help us remember that our greatest power is in our agreement with you. Amen.

We can understand these things,
for we have the mind of Christ.

1 Corinthians 2:16 NLT

A Common Purpose

*The one who plants
and the one who waters
have a common purpose,
and each will receive
wages according to
the labor of each.*
1 Corinthians 3:8 NRSV

What would your marriage look like if the two of you were alike? What if you shared every opinion, every skill, and every talent? That just wouldn't work, would it? For one thing, you would quickly become bored with each other, and for another, you wouldn't get much accomplished.

God has given each of you your own unique gifts and talents. He formed your brains and bequeathed to each of you the privilege of free thought. You are to complement rather than conform to each other. Working together, your differences become assets.

Unity does not mean being carbon copies of each other. It means appreciating and using your various gifts to accomplish God's purposes.

We thank you, God, for the diversity you've placed in our marriage. Help us to use our gifts for a common purpose. Amen.

Let the favor of the
Lord our God be
upon us, and prosper
for us the work of
our hands!

Psalm 90:17 NRSV

Blessed Harmony

Harmony is as refreshing as the dew from Mount Hermon that falls on the mountains of Zion.

Psalm 133:3 NLT

If you've been married for more than a day, you almost certainly know how bad it feels to be out of step with each other. It is stressful for your minds and bodies. That lack of harmony also short-circuits your ability to enjoy the blessings God has poured out on you.

God's commandments, his instruction, and his laws are not born from a heady ego. He isn't a bully. Just like any good father, his concern is for his children. Understand that he loves you and wants you to enjoy all the good things this life has to offer. His instruction to live together in harmony is intended to help you avoid stress and live your lives to the fullest.

God, when we struggle to make unity
a reality in our lives, we agree to
put what you want first. Amen.

Beloved, I pray that all may go well with
you and that you may be in good health,
just as it is well with your soul.

3 John 1:2 NRSV

Honoring Peace

It is good and pleasant when God's people live together in peace!

Psalm 133:1 NCV

∞

Nothing can keep you from fulfilling your God-given purpose, but discord can diminish its impact and rob you and others of the effectiveness of your gifts.

Imagine yourselves as pianists performing before an audience of music lovers. Throughout the performance, one or both of you keep hitting the wrong note. Though the vast majority of the notes are right on, the audience is distracted by the few that are not, and the impact and enjoyment of the music is all but lost.

The piece God has given you to play is much too beautiful to be marred by jarring notes of discord. A clean performance takes patience and practice, but the symphony of peace that results makes it all worthwhile.

～

God, help us as we strive to eliminate the wrong notes and make our lives the beautiful music you intended them to be. Amen.

*I will hear what God the L*ORD *will
speak, for He will speak peace to
His people and to His saints.*

Psalm 85:8 NKJV

Beautiful Music

We have gifts that differ according to the grace given to us.

Romans 12:6 NRSV

Some people make the mistake of thinking that harmony means joining the crowd or conforming to what other people think. Actually, just the opposite is true. Harmony means that you choose to do the right thing for the right reasons and for the mutual good.

An instrument played alone has a compelling sound, but when played as part of an orchestra, it takes on an added richness. Interestingly, each instrument brings its own special sound to the whole, and each holds a place in the composition that would be empty without it.

The songs you play to each other are good, but add to them the magnificence of the greater score.

God, we come to you with hearts humbled.
We yearn to be part of what you are
doing in the earth. Amen.

We are happy because of the hope we
have of sharing God's glory.

Romans 5:2 NCV

Love Rules

Clothe yourselves with love, which binds everything together in perfect harmony.

Colossians 3:14 NRSV

The key to harmony is love—pure and simple. Without it, all your efforts to walk together in peace will fall flat. Love is the only thing on earth powerful enough to motivate you to lay aside what you want in favor of what is best for others.

There are many kinds of love, but only one kind makes all the others work. Agape love, the love God has for you and the love you have for him, is the preeminent factor that will bind you together in the way God intends.

When you struggle to give up your way and walk in unity, remember what God has given up for you. That will give you encouragement to keep going.

God, help us as we endeavor to lay aside our self-centered ways and focus on coming together in honor of your great love. Amen.

*Let us lay aside every weight . . .
and let us run with endurance
the race that is set before us.*

Hebrews 12:1 NKJV

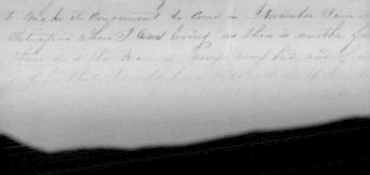

Faithfulness

Do not let loyalty and faithfulness forsake you; bind them around your neck, write them on the tablet of your heart.

Proverbs 3:3 NRSV

A Faithful Example

*Our LORD, you keep
your word and do
everything you say.*
Psalm 145:13 CEV

Perhaps you've been to Yellowstone National Park and seen the geyser they call Old Faithful. It is so named because it shoots water up into the air with amazing regularity, and it has done this for as long as anyone can remember. It's dependable. If you were to go there to see it, you would surely be rewarded.

God is much more dependable than any geyser. Go to him, and you will not be disappointed —ever! He keeps all his promises.

Faithfulness in life, and especially in marriage, is imperative. You must be able to depend on each other. Follow God's example as each of you strive to be someone the other can rely on.

God, help us to learn from your example to
be faithful to you, to each other, and to
others in the world around us. Amen.

*All the ways of the Lord are
loving and faithful.*

Psalm 25:10 NIV

A Faithful Provision

God will meet all your needs according to his glorious riches in Christ Jesus.

Philippians 4:19 NIV

God is a good father and a faithful provider for his children. When you go to him with your needs, you can be confident that he hears you and will make a way for your needs to be met.

Of course, you should know that God works in mysterious ways. Your provision may not come in the form you are expecting, but it will come in the form God feels is best. He is God, and it is his call to make.

If you have a need today—and who doesn't—take it to God in prayer. He is able to provide for you from his vast resources. And he is faithful. You can count on that.

We come before you with our requests,
God, and we ask for your provision.
We thank you because we know you
are completely faithful. Amen.

"My people will be satisfied with My goodness," declares the L ORD.

Jeremiah 31:14 NASB

God Is Listening

The LORD has set apart the faithful for himself; the LORD hears when I call to him.

Psalm 4:3 NRSV

∞

When two people love each other, they spend hours listening to each other, strengthening that connection between them. You might think that after a while they would grow tired, but their love renews them. They can't get enough.

The same is true with God. He is always eager to hear what you have to say. You aren't an inconvenience to him or an interruption in his divine thoughts. He will listen as long as you are speaking, and even then he will listen to the unspoken language of your heart.

Spend time talking to God. Share with him your thoughts and opinions. Ask him the questions you want to know the answers to. He is a faithful listener.

We pour out our hearts to you, God,
and we do so with the confidence
that you hear every word. Amen.

*I will pray to the L<small>ORD</small>, and he will answer
me from his holy mountain.*

Psalm 3:4 NCV

A Call to Fellowship

God is faithful; by him you were called into the fellowship of his Son, Jesus Christ our Lord.

1 Corinthians 1:9 NRSV

Have you ever asked yourself where you would be without the kindness and faithfulness of God? It's good to think about that sometimes because it forces you to recognize all he has done for you.

God knows your hearts, and he sees you as you really are. When you make mistakes—and all human beings do—he lifts you up, cleans you off, and reminds you that you belong to a royal family. What a miracle of grace, what a gift of unspeakable value.

Go to God, raise your hands together, and offer him your thanks and praises. Let him know how much you appreciate being his child. Thank him for his faithfulness.

God, we thank you for faithfully loving us through all our difficulties. We will not forget what you've done for us. Amen.

He destined us for adoption as his
children through Jesus Christ, according
to the good pleasure of his will.

Ephesians 1:5 NRSV

A Faithful Heritage

The LORD is good; his steadfast love endures forever, and his faithfulness to all generations.

Psalm 100:5 NRSV

∞

If you make a commitment for a week, you might have no trouble faithfully carrying through. But make that same commitment for a year or even two years, and staying faithful becomes a great deal more difficult.

God does not struggle with faithfulness in this way. He is not restricted by time and space. He doesn't grow tired of doing what needs to be done. He is certain to keep his promises to you today, tomorrow, and forever. God is eternally faithful, never faltering.

When you place your trust in him, he will never let you down. You can count on him no matter what circumstance you might encounter. He will always be there for you.

∞

God, we place our trust in your great faithfulness. Thank you for the stability you bring to our lives in the midst of a confused and faithless world. Amen.

Those who trust in the Lord are as Mount Zion,
which cannot be moved but abides forever.

Psalm 125:1 NASB

God Is Right and True

The LORD is truthful;
he can be trusted.
Psalm 33:4 CEV

∞

At one time or another, you've probably made a commitment or a promise that you thought better of later. Maybe you didn't think it through carefully enough or you realized you didn't have all the information you needed. Your humanness interferes with your faithfulness.

But God's promises are always right and true. Because he sees all and knows all, he doesn't make mistakes in judgment. His commitment to love and care for the two of you cannot be breached or revoked. He won't decide tomorrow that you are too much trouble.

You can depend on that as you lie down to sleep at night. You won't awaken the next day to find that God has changed his mind. What wonderful peace of mind that brings.

God, we thank you for your unwavering love.
We owe our lives, our marriage, and
everything we have to you. Amen.

*When God wanted to guarantee his
promises, he gave his word, a rock-solid
guarantee—God can't break his word.*

Hebrews 6:18 MSG

A Faithful Exchange

*To the faithful you show
yourself faithful.*
2 Samuel 22:26 NIV
∞

If meditating on God's faithfulness motivates you, it should be to make you more faithful to each other. Too often cultural messages serve to diminish love as something that doesn't last forever. When it's over, these messages say, you should just move on and start up again with someone else.

But that philosophy is opposed to the principle learned from God's faithfulness. He never gives up on those he loves. He remains faithful no matter what.

When the two of you hit a bump in your relationship and you wonder if you should go on, consider God's standard of faithfulness. Let it inspire you to keep working to resolve your differences and fall in love again.

God, we thank you for your worthy example of faithfulness and ask that you help us as we strive to walk in your footsteps. Amen.

God Is Your Faithful Defender

*The Lord is faithful,
who will establish
you and guard you
from the evil one.*

2 Thessalonians 3:3 NKJV

Dead bolts, car alarms, firearms, security systems, seat belts—those are just a few of the tools you may be using to try to keep yourselves and your possessions safe from the evil in the world. But what are you doing to keep your souls safe from the evil one, the one who wants to destroy you because you belong to God?

The Bible urges vigilance with regard to your enemy, the devil. But you need not be afraid. He is all smoke and mirrors. You won't be vulnerable to his wily schemes as long as you are tuned in to God, who is the faithful guardian of your souls. When you call on him, the evil one will flee.

God, we thank you for keeping us safe from the enemy of our souls. We will be wise by being unafraid of his wily schemes. Amen.

Submit therefore to God. Resist the devil and he will flee from you.

James 4:7 NASB

Cultivating Faithfulness

Trust in the Lord and do good; dwell in the land and cultivate faithfulness.

Psalm 37:3 NASB

Faithfulness is a wonderful virtue, and one that comes from the Holy Spirit as you become more familiar with the ways of God. Still, faithfulness does not become imbedded in your life without practice.

Make all your commitments thoughtfully and prayerfully. Speak them aloud to each other or write them down. Then agree to be watchdogs for each other. Give the encouragement needed to follow through when inconvenience and second thoughts come to bear. And understand that even the smallest commitments are important.

If you are diligent, faithfulness will become part of your character and a way of life for you. And you will become more and more like God.

God, we want to be faithful to you, to each other, and to others. We want our lives to be characterized by faithfulness as we live by your example. Amen.

*If you make a promise to God, don't be slow
to keep it.... Give God what you promised.*

Ecclesiastes 5:4 NCV

Put to the Test

It is required that those who have been given a trust must prove faithful.

1 Corinthians 4:2 NIV

You can be certain that every time you make a commitment, give your word, or make a promise, it will be tested. For example, your promise to spend time together on the weekend will be tested by an unexpected invitation to go shopping or play golf.

Being faithful, even in the day-to-day commitments you make to each other, is important. It teaches you to be thoughtful about what commitments you make, and it helps you establish a pattern of faithfulness in your lives.

Faithfulness is worth all the sacrifices it requires and all the inconvenience it causes because it will strengthen and discipline you in every area of your lives.

God, we want to be faithful in matters great and small. Help us as we make commitments and put ourselves to the test. Amen.

He who is faithful in
what is least is faithful
also in much.

Luke 16:10 NKJV

The Blessings of Faithfulness

The trustworthy person will get a rich reward.
Proverbs 28:20 NLT

Faithfulness is one of the more difficult virtues. It often calls for discipline, self-control, and sacrifice. But like so many of the things God calls you to, the cultivation of faithfulness brings with it abundant rewards.

Along with the satisfaction of knowing you are pleasing God, you will find a deeper level of trust in your marriage. You will gain the respect and appreciation of those you encounter each day. And your lives, in general, will be more settled, more productive, and more satisfying.

Many people miss the blessings of faithfulness because they underestimate its importance in the little things of life. But if you are willing to work hard at it, your lives will be changed forever.

God, we are eager to receive the blessings
that come with faithfulness. Thank you
for your goodness to us. Amen.

I will cause showers to come down in their season; they will be showers of blessing.

Ezekiel 34:26 *NASB*

The Fruit of Faithfulness

The Holy Spirit produces this kind of fruit in our lives: love, joy, peace, patience, kindness, goodness, faithfulness, gentleness, and self-control.

Galatians 5:22–23 NLT

The Holy Spirit is a virtue builder. Because he is always with you, living inside you, he is always working to help you become the person you were created to be. With the Holy Spirit's gentle tutelage, you will grow not only in faithfulness but also in many of God's most endearing characteristics. In other words, you will grow more like him.

In addition to faithfulness, you will also be blessed with love, joy, peace, patience, kindness, goodness, gentleness, and self-control. Imagine what a marriage that will make.

God has so much in store for the two of you. Keep your hearts open to the work of the Holy Spirit, and soon you will be reaping a harvest of godliness.

God, we invite your Holy Spirit to work in us. If we grow weary along the way, we welcome your lesson on faithfulness. Amen.

If we live by the Spirit,
let us also walk by the Spirit.

Galatians 5:25 NASB

A Life of Faithfulness

You will have loyal friends if you want to do right.

Proverbs 14:22 CEV

God's plan for the two of you is more than an act of faithfulness or a period of faithfulness; it is a life of faithfulness. His intention is for you to live it every day. He does this because he loves you and wishes to spare you the pain that comes with faithlessness.

God is not an egotist, suggesting that you jump through hoops for his own entertainment. He wants to see your marriage succeed and your lives awash with blessing. He wants good things for you throughout your lives.

Agree together to see the goodness of God's plan. You will find that it is a life lived to the fullest.

God, we know you want what is best for us.
We ask you to help us as we embark on
the adventure of godliness. Amen.

*See how very much our Father loves us, for he
calls us his children, and that is what we are!*

1 John 3:1 NLT

Faithful All the Way

If you remain faithful even when facing death, I will give you the crown of life.
Revelation 2:10 NLT

Have either of you ever said, "Darling, I love you more than my life"? Even if you didn't say it just that way, you probably understand the sentiment. At some point, your love transcended earthly definition and became fully sacrificial and divine.

Of course, the odds of your ever having to make that daunting choice are remote, and the momentary intense feeling of love that brought on the remark might not fully stand up in the light of reality. But that love is a glimpse of the kind of love God has for you. He is utterly faithful. He loved you more than his own life. This is the gold standard for love and faithfulness.

God, we thank you for demonstrating what
love and faithfulness are all about
by giving your life for us. Amen.

I will sing your praises among the nations. For your unfailing love is as high as the heavens. You faithfulness reaches to the clouds.

Psalm 57:9–10 NLT

The Award of Faithfulness

Well done, good and faithful servant! You have been faithful with a few things; I will put you in charge of many things.

Matthew 25:21 NIV

The highest decoration awarded by the U.S. government is the Medal of Honor. Fewer than thirty-five hundred men and women have received the award since 1861, when the award was authorized by President Abraham Lincoln. It is given for conspicuous gallantry beyond the call of duty. Imagine what it would be like to receive such an award.

The Bible says that one of the highest decorations awarded in the kingdom of God is for faithfulness. It is the award for the accomplishment of God's purpose and plan for your lives. Now picture in your mind what it would be like to receive that award from God! Faithfulness is your highest calling.

God, we ask for the help of your Holy Spirit as we endeavor to learn to make faithfulness a primary characteristic of our lives. Amen.

*My eyes shall be on the faithful of the land,
that they may dwell with me.*

Psalm 101:6 NKJV

Purpose

∾

God is working in you to make you
willing and able to obey him.

Philippians 2:13 CEV

God's Purpose for You

The plans of the LORD stand firm forever; the purposes of his heart through all generations.
Psalm 33:11 NIV

God has a purpose for your lives, and to that end, he has devised a plan that will draw out all your gifts and refine your personalities and temperaments. This plan is more like a blueprint than a set-in-stone directive. It allows for your own creative ideas and passions. It makes allowances for personal choices and even mistakes.

The purpose at the end of each plan is for you to become the people God created you to be. The inner work he does in your hearts and minds will one day cause a stir in the world around you. You could say that God makes a difference in the world, one changed person at a time.

God, we desire your purpose for our lives. Therefore, we ask you to reveal your plan to us, one day at a time. Amen.

*God causes everything to work together for
the good of those who love God and are called
according to his purpose for them.*

Romans 8:28 NLT

Created for Good Works

We are His workmanship, created in Christ Jesus for good works, which God prepared beforehand that we should walk in them.

Ephesians 2:10 NKJV

God's purpose and plan for every person, including what he has in mind for the two of you, has one significant characteristic in common. Each is inherently good. His plan is never deceitful or manipulative. It contains no greedy or egocentric motives. And though there are sometimes painful elements involved, God's plan never creates useless suffering. Its outcome is always, in a word, good.

Goodness is an attribute of God and the very adjective he used to describe his initial work of creation. Like a builder who is careful to use only materials of the highest quality, God has a plan for your life that is good in every way. Without a doubt, it will bring great blessing to your lives.

God, we would expect nothing less from you than an entirely good plan for our lives. We step into it enthusiastically. Amen.

*The Lord is good.... He leads the humble in
doing right, teaching them his way.*

Psalm 25:8–9 NLT

Working the Plan

Work out your salvation with fear and trembling.

Philippians 2:12 NASB

Think of God's plan for your lives as a set of working instructions implanted into your brains before you were even placed in your mothers' wombs. God is the author of those plans, but you are the facilitators.

No one but you can fulfill God's plans for you. They were created specifically for the unique creations you are. And it is your duty and your privilege to throw all your strength and passion into them.

This might sound daunting, but God has sent you a helper, the Holy Spirit, who is as close as your thoughts and who understands your plan from start to finish. Together you will build a couple of spectacular masterpieces.

God, we commit ourselves to work
faithfully toward the fulfillment of
your plan for our lives. Amen.

[God said:] *"Before I formed you in the womb I knew you, and before you were born I consecrated you."*

Jeremiah 1:5 NASB

By His Power

We constantly pray for you, that our God may count you worthy of his calling, and that by his power he may fulfill every good purpose of yours.

2 Thessalonians 1:11 NIV

It's probable that for as long as you can remember, you have each had a dream percolating in your hearts. That dream is part of God's plan for you. He placed it inside you to motivate you to pursue his purpose for your lives.

There is one significant difference, however, between the dream you see and the one he sees for you. God's dream for you is the finished product, the actual prize at the end of your life story. The dream you see is just the rough stone. You could say it is like a diamond with its luster still hidden. You will behold more and more of its beauty as you pursue it under God's guiding hand.

God, we are so grateful for the dream that is being revealed within each of us. We look to you to guide us through the process. Amen.

He puts a little of heaven in our hearts
so that we'll never settle for less.
2 Corinthians 5:5 MSG

Noble Purposes

God is an amazing facilitator who gets the most out of everything he does. No circumstance, no insight, no obstacle, not even your mistakes will be wasted. He will use a situation in your lives to strengthen and encourage someone else. And he will use someone else's struggles and lessons learned to strengthen and encourage you.

This is true with those outside your marriage relationship, but it is especially true as the two of you interact as husband and wife. God will use the two of you to teach, motivate, and inspire each other. And he will use each of you to strengthen and encourage others. What a wise and resourceful God he is.

God, help us to become fitting vessels to be
used for your good purpose in our own
lives and the lives of others. Amen.

Let us cleanse ourselves
... And let us work
toward complete holiness
because we fear God.

2 Corinthians 7:1 NLT

Knowing God's Will

Always be joyful. Never stop praying. Be thankful in all circumstances, for this is God's will for you who belong to Christ Jesus.

1 Thessalonians 5:16–18
NLT

∞

Finding the will of God may sound daunting, but in reality, it is like unlocking pieces of a puzzle that has always been inside you. While it is a process of discovery, in a sense, it is discovering something you've always known.

It's normal to have a few miscues early on, but at some point you will find yourself face-to-face with something that strikes a chord within you. God's will for you might be an expansion of something you're already doing. Or it could be something you are trying for the first time. Either way, you will know you've found it.

The will of God is not some big mystery. God's will for you is a natural progression of the things you do with joy every day.

∞

God, we want your will for our lives
separately and together. Give us insight
as we endeavor to find the puzzle pieces
and put them in place. Amen.

I delight to do your will, O my God;
your law is within my heart.

Psalm 40:8 NRSV

Trusting God's Plan

I know the plans I have for you, says the LORD, plans for your welfare and not for harm, to give you a future with hope.

Jeremiah 29:11 NRSV

Some people struggle against God's plan and purpose for their lives because they think it will mean they can't do the things they want to do. If this is how you are feeling, be assured that God has no desire to trick you into doing something that will make you miserable. He simply wants you to know who you really are. His plan will always dovetail with that revelation.

God isn't the author of discord and confusion. He loves you and wants good things for both of you. When you can begin to trust him and allow his will to unfold before you, you will only wonder why you waited so long to discover such a beautiful gift.

God, we gladly lay down our notions of what is good for us, and we eagerly wait to see your will unfold before us. Amen.

How great is your goodness that you have stored up for those who fear you, that you have given to those who trust you.

Psalm 31:19 NCV

Everything Has a Purpose

The LORD has made everything for his own purposes, even the wicked.

Proverbs 16:4 NLT

Have you ever suffered a setback and wondered what purpose the experience might have? You are right to question, because God wastes nothing—not one tear, not one heartache, and not one outrageous blunder. No matter what senseless circumstance you might encounter, he will extract from it some purpose, some benefit that will help you reach your goal of becoming the people he has created you to be.

Comfort yourselves with this. In your sorrows, he instills wells of compassion. From your mistakes, he teaches wisdom and understanding. And in your darkest hour, he assures you that he will never leave you nor forsake you. He will always be right by your side.

Thank you, God, for seeing that even our troubles and tragedies work some kind of good in our lives. We trust you. Amen.

You, O Lord, are a God full of compassion,
and gracious, longsuffering and
abundant in mercy and truth.

Psalm 86:15 NKJV

It Shall Be

The LORD of hosts has sworn: As I have designed, so shall it be; and as I have planned, so shall it come to pass.

Isaiah 14:24 NRSV

You might think that the way you have lived so far has spoiled God's plan and purpose for your lives. But when you think that way, you wrongly conclude that God has been defeated. He is not capable of carrying out his plan and purpose. This could not be further from the truth.

God has seen all the detours and bunny trails you have taken through the years. He saw them long ago and created his plan accordingly. Of course, you have missed the joy and blessings those years could have brought you, but God's overall plan cannot be deterred. The moment you turn back to him, he will set your feet once again on the path to his purpose.

God, we thank you for the indestructible plan you have created for our lives. Set our feet once again upon the path. Amen.

He has saved me from death, my eyes
from tears, my feet from stumbling.

Psalm 116:8 NLT

∞

Purposing in Your Hearts

We want to do what pleases the Lord and what people think is right.

2 Corinthians 8:21 CEV

When God created you, he established his will and purpose in your hearts. It would have been an easy task to push some buttons and send you off to accomplish that purpose. However, God was determined that unlike the angels and his other creations, you would receive a remarkable gift that would place you in a special category shared only with God himself.

God has given each of you the ability to make your own choices. He did this because he did not want to mandate your love or demand your fellowship. He longed to be freely loved, freely trusted, and freely obeyed.

God has granted you the choice. Will you purpose in your heart to agree with his will for you?

God, we thank you for the gift of free will that you bestowed on us. It is a blessing and a responsibility we do not take lightly. Amen.

You have been called to live in freedom....
Use your freedom to serve one another in love.

Galatians 5:13 NLT

Pleasing God

Some people take exception with the idea that they should commit their lives to pleasing God. Who is he, anyway? And why does he think everyone should please him?

Those would seem like fair questions if it were not for this. God's purpose for you is that you succeed in every way, that you be blessed and prosperous and well in mind, soul, and body. He wants to see you fulfill your potential and become the best two people you can be.

Pleasing God is not about inflating his ego. Like a coach who looks out for his players, he wants to see you win. When you purpose to please the Lord, you are purposing to please yourselves.

God, we trust you to help us become the best we can be as we purpose in our hearts to please you. Amen.

We didn't speak to please people, but to please God who knows our motives.

1 Thessalonians 2:4 CEV

Making His Purpose Yours

I do not mean that I am already as God wants me to be. I have not yet reached that goal, but I continue trying to reach it and to make it mine.

Philippians 3:12 NCV

∞

Fulfilling God's purpose and plan can be a little like going to college. You will have times of intense learning where your focus is fully occupied. You will also have periods of rest and times of refreshing.

Fulfilling God's purpose will take you a lifetime, but you will succeed one class at a time, and you will acquire wisdom, understanding, and knowledge all along the way. When you reach heaven and hear him say "Well done," you will have received your degree.

One day you will look back on your lives and realize that finding God's purpose is primarily about a joyful journey—one with a fabulous celebration of your achievement at the end.

God, we want to take the joyous journey of discovery and fulfillment that will reveal the people you created us to be. Amen.

I am certain that God, who began the good work within you, will continue his work until it is finally finished on the day when Christ Jesus returns.

Philippians 1:6 NLT

Fully Committed

May He grant you according to your heart's desire, and fulfill all your purpose.
Psalm 20:4 NKJV
∞

When you set out to fulfill God's purpose for your lives, you must be determined to get there. Think of it this way: If you wish to go to a certain city, you get on the highway and head in that direction. If you turn off at every attractive venue along the way, you might never reach your destination.

God has much in store for you, more than you can ever imagine. It eclipses anything you can possibly encounter along the way.

Dismiss distractions and set your heart on the things of God. Be determined to fulfill your purpose, and God will see that nothing on earth will keep you from reaching your destination.

∼

God, we set our hearts on fulfilling your purpose;
help us to clearly see distractions for what
they are and stay the course. Amen.

*Oh, that my steps might be steady,
keeping to the course you set.*

Psalm 119:5 MSG

Why You Are Here

It's in Christ that we find out who we are and what we are living for.

Ephesians 1:12 MSG

Some people think our presence here is just a big cosmic coincidence; therefore, nothing really matters. Those people would encourage you to enjoy your life as much as possible and then surrender to the darkness and oblivion.

What a sad scenario that is, and far from the truth. The universe and all that is within it did not just happen. God created it with a grand purpose in mind. He also created you and carefully placed you in the midst of it. Everything matters, because everything—good and bad—pushes you either closer to or further away from what God intends for you.

Close your ears to such nonsense and set out together on the great adventure of finding God's purpose for your lives.

God, we will not listen to those who foolishly dismiss your power and majesty. Go with us as we embark on the greatest adventure of our lives. Amen.

We have received God's Spirit (not the
world's spirit), so we can know the wonderful
things God has freely given us.

1 Corinthians 2:12 NLT

Discovery

When you call upon me and come and
pray to me, I will hear you. When you
search for me, you will find me; if you
seek me with all your heart.

Jeremiah 29:12–13 NRSV

Finding Rest

Ask for the old, godly way, and walk in it. Travel its path, and you will find rest for your souls.

Jeremiah 6:16 NLT

∽

Do you wonder when the madness of daily life will stop long enough for you to catch your breath? If you are, as most people, caught up in this schedule-obsessed society, you fall into bed at night exhausted and wondering if you're too tired to sleep.

You're right to think God wants you to tend to business and meet your responsibilities, but he also means for you to enjoy your life and treat your body like the holy temple it is. Rest isn't a luxury; it's a necessity. Without it, your body will be vulnerable to disease and even premature death. Physical rest will come more readily when you release your cares to God. Then, finally, you'll be able to catch your breath again.

∽

God, we ask for the rest that comes when
we allow you to help us shoulder our
daily responsibilities. Amen.

On the seventh day...
God rested from all his work.

Genesis 2:2 *NLT*

Finding Grace

Let us therefore approach the throne of grace with boldness, so that we may receive mercy and find grace to help in time of need.

Hebrews 4:16 NRSV

God's grace—his undeserved favor—applies to every aspect of your lives. Think of it this way: God's grace makes your path wider than your feet. That means if you stumble, you will have room to catch yourself. God makes allowances for you. You don't have to worry; he already knows you aren't perfect.

The question is, do the two of you minister grace to each other? Do you each allow for the other's mistakes? Open your hearts to receive grace freely from the hand of God and extend it just as freely to each other. Consider it a gift, for that's what it is—undeserved and unearned. Grace is a gift that will bless you in return.

God, we are grateful that you cover our mistakes with your love. Help us as we learn to extend grace to each other. Amen.

How rich is God's grace, which he has given to us so fully and freely.

Ephesians 1:7–8 NCV

Finding Understanding

Who is wise and under-standing among you? Let him show it by his good life, by deeds done in the humility that comes from wisdom.

James 3:13 NIV

When you think about it, marriage is an impossible task. Imagine the degree of difficulty involved when two people, though deeply in love, bring together differing temperaments, personalities, intellects, backgrounds, and all the other complexities that define human beings. And yet, from the beginning marriage was God's idea.

Perhaps he knew that the powerful gravitational pull of love would motivate couples to learn the virtues of goodness, understanding, humility, and wisdom. He might also have reasoned that two people faced with such an impossible task would turn their eyes to the one for whom nothing is impossible.

If you need understanding in your relationship, open your hearts to him, and he will help you find your way.

God, we ask you to help us better understand each other and understand how your presence in our marriage can make it stronger and more productive. Amen.

To get wisdom is to love oneself; to keep understanding is to prosper.

Proverbs 19:8 NRSV

Finding Strength

A person standing alone can be attacked and defeated, but two can stand back-to-back and conquer. Three are even better, for a triple-braided cord is not easily broken.

Ecclesiastes 4:12 NLT

∞

When two people stand and face the world together, they have an obvious advantage over those who stand alone. Like two strands of a rope woven together, they become stronger, better able to deal with the extremities of everyday life. Burdens are lighter when shared, dilemmas less baffling, and suffering less intense.

Now, imagine adding God to that equation. Your strength, power, courage, and understanding would be multiplied exponentially, and you would have the benefit of his wisdom and guidance. In fact, everything you have together would be enhanced.

Agree to ask God to be part of your marriage. His presence will make your bond, like a three-stranded cord, virtually unbreakable.

∾

God, we invite you to be a vital part of our
relationship, empowering us to be
the best we can be. Amen.

Please, LORD, be kind to us! We depend on
you. Make us strong each morning, and come
to save us when we are in trouble.

Isaiah 33:2 CEV

Discovering the Ways of the Spirit

Humans can reproduce only human life, but the Holy Spirit gives birth to spiritual life.

John 3:6 NLT

Inviting God into your relationship implies a commitment to get to know him better and seek out his ways. If you have the idea that doing so would be boring and all about "religion," think again. Discovering your faith is one of the most exciting adventures you will ever undertake—and the two of you have the opportunity to embark on that journey hand in hand.

You'll be amazed as you seek God in prayer and see his answers become reality in your lives. Within the pages of the Bible, you will find mind-blowing insights about your relationship to God, to others, and to each other. Brace yourselves for the ride of your lives.

God, we thank you for the opportunity to learn more about you and your ways. Walk with us hand in hand through life. Amen.

*He who raised Christ from the dead
will also bring your mortal bodies to life
through His Spirit who lives in you.*

Romans 8:11 HCSB

Solving the Divine Mystery

While the particulars of faith are straightforward, mystery shrouds the whys of relationship with God. Why would almighty God choose to love us, and how can his greatness be reconciled with our smallness?

The mystery of God's love for you and his determination to be part of your lives is one that will unfold over a lifetime. If the reality of God's presence in your lives came all at once, you would not be able to bear the glorious nature of it all.

God's desire to be present in you as well as with you is a wonder and delight you have the privilege of sharing, and one that will continue in this life and the next.

∼

God, we are so grateful for your presence in our lives. We are in awe of the great mystery of your love for us. Amen.

In Him we live and move and exist, as
even some of your own poets have said,
"For we also are His children."

Acts 17:28 NASB

Searching for Revelation

May the name of God be praised forever and ever. … He reveals the deep and hidden things.
Daniel 2:20, 22 HCSB

Some people are obsessed with revelation. They want to have the inside track, be in on what's coming down the road. The truth is that God has only given us glimpses of what the future holds—and for a reason. Would you really want to know what will happen tomorrow? Could you deal with it if you did know?

As a couple, determine to trust God for what is coming in the future. You won't be walking in the dark. The light of his presence will brightly light the path just ahead of your feet. Take hands, and then take his hand. He is all the revelation you will ever need.

God, we believe that you will tell us everything we need to know. We take your hand and place our trust in your faithfulness. Amen.

This I pray, that your love may abound still more
and more in real knowledge and all discernment.

Philippians 1:9 NASB

Your Unknowable God

No one can discover everything God is doing under the sun. Not even the wisest people discover everything.

Ecclesiastes 8:17 NLT

∞

Close your eyes for a moment and think about God. Imagine as best you can the vastness of his creation, the universe and beyond. Consider the terms *omniscient, omnipresent, omnipotent*—"all knowing," "always present," and "all powerful." That's who God is. Then think for a moment about his love for you and about how he intervenes in human affairs. Even eternity would not offer enough time to know him completely. He is unknowable.

But being unknowable does not mean God cannot be known. Each day you have an opportunity to know him better. Each day you can learn something new and wonderful about who he is and what he does. Determine to find out all you can about your unknowable God.

∾

God, we thank you for allowing us to know
you, our unknowable God, better
and better each day. Amen.

*Thanks be to God, who in Christ always
leads us in triumphal procession, and
through us spreads in every place the
fragrance that comes from knowing him.*

2 Corinthians 2:14 NRSV

Discovering the Scriptures

Whatever things were written before were written for our learning, that we through the patience and comfort of the Scriptures might have hope.

Romans 15:4 NKJV

The Bible has been described as God's love letter to humankind. Imagine that. God saw fit to write you a letter, filled with information about himself and the wonderful plans he has for each of you.

So deep, reflective, and beautiful is this letter in book form that you will find new insights every time you read it. In the first books of the Bible, God provides a glimpse of how everything came to be. The book of Psalms reveals God's heart, while the book of Proverbs uncovers his wisdom. The Gospels introduce you to God the Son— Jesus—and the epistles unveil his dreams for his children. You'll want to read this letter repeatedly.

God, we thank you for your love letter, the Bible. We open our hearts to hear you speak to us as we read your words. Amen.

Jesus said, "The words that I speak to you are spirit, and they are life."

John 6:63 NKJV

Discovering Each Other

Some people marry and then years later realize they don't really know each other. It's sad but understandable. Falling in love focuses on surface issues like physical attraction, looks, and charm. The kind of love that makes a marriage strong and resilient is based on a deep knowledge, understanding, and acceptance of the real person inside.

Even if the two of you married knowing only the superficial kind of love, you can still pursue a richer, deeper relationship. Set aside time to talk about your dreams, and practice trusting each other with your secret hopes and fears. Learn to know each other as friends. Your journey of discovery will open up levels of intimacy you never imagined possible.

We want a marriage that will last. Help us, God, as we work to know each other better, and give us joy in the journey. Amen.

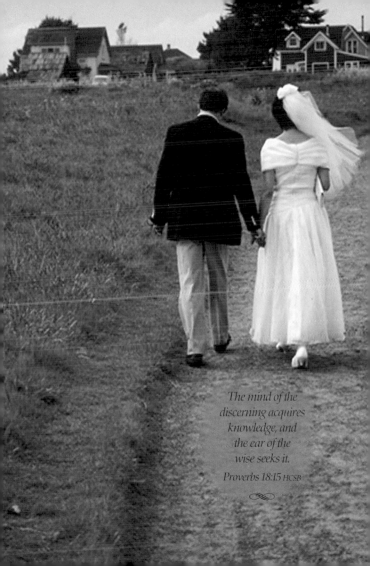

The mind of the
discerning acquires
knowledge, and
the ear of the
wise seeks it.

Proverbs 18:15 HCSB

Finding the Path for Your Lives

Teach us to number our days aright, that we may gain a heart of wisdom.

Psalm 90:12 NIV

Life is funny. Most people say searching for their path in life is difficult and challenging. It often requires hard work and persistence. And emotions often run high. *Will I find what I'm looking for? Is there really something out there for me?* The interesting thing is that when people get older, they often look back on that time of searching as some of the best years of their lives.

If you are just beginning your search, take time to enjoy the process. If you are almost at the end of your path, enjoy what you've already found, but don't stop seeking. Keep your mind sharp and your spiritual senses honed. There is still much to discover along the way.

God, we thank you for helping us find the right path for our feet. Guide us as we discover all you have in mind for us. Amen.

When you get serious about finding me and want it more than anything else, I'll make sure you won't be disappointed.

Jeremiah 29:13 MSG

Imagining Wonders to Come

No eye has seen, no ear has heard, and no mind has imagined what God has prepared for those who love him.

1 Corinthians 2:9 NLT

Nothing you see or hear in this life can prepare you for what God has in store for you in heaven. The little bit the Bible reveals greatly emphasizes the beauty and grandeur of living near the foot of God's throne in heavenly places. But the human mind is unable to fathom the wonder of it all.

Think of the best thing either of you have ever experienced—the most beautiful sunset, the most delicious food, the most refreshing swim, the most exciting sports event, the most relaxing vacation, the most inviting home. That's what heaven will be like, and so much more. Spending eternity with God is a journey to your imagination and beyond.

God, we are in awe of you. We can't wait to
see what you have in store for us when
we leave this world. Amen.

He has put eternity in their
hearts, except that no one can
find out the work that God
does from beginning to end.

Ecclesiastes 3:11 NKJV

Endurance

∞

Let us run with endurance the race that
is set before us, looking unto Jesus, the
author and finisher of our faith.

Hebrews 12:1–2 NKJV

Working for the Reward

Don't get tired of helping others. You will be rewarded when the time is right, if you don't give up.

Galatians 6:9 CEV

You may think it's crass to expect a reward for doing good. Isn't that something that should be done from a pure motive? Shouldn't you be doing good things because God has done so many good things for you? Of course, you're right—but the fact is, a reward is waiting!

God knows human nature. He understands how easy it is to get distracted, tired, and frustrated. He realizes human beings often begin with good motives and then give up when the going gets tough. Perhaps that's why he holds that reward out there—something extra to get us through the hard places and motivate us to continue sharing his goodness with others.

God, you reward us in so many ways. Just having you in our lives is a reward. Thank you for being so good to us. Amen.

Do not throw away this confident trust in the Lord. Remember the great reward it brings you!

Hebrews 10:35 NLT

Standing Strong

If you pay close attention to what's happening around you, it's easy to lose perspective. Horrors like AIDS, famine, wars, brutal dictators, oppression, and the evil that preys on the poor and powerless seem to be closing in on every side.

But one truth eclipses all the pain, suffering, and injustice. God brings light and hope to a dark, hopeless world. He is faithful and true in a world filled with selfishness and deceit. He is the one person you can count on; he is the one person who will never let you down.

The next time you feel like the world is closing in, look up. Keep your eyes fixed on God. That's where your hope and strength will come from.

God, we will not relinquish our hope to the evil in this world. We will trust in you. When we grow faith—and we will—strengthen us. Amen.

We are hard-pressed on every side, yet not crushed; we are perplexed, but not in despair; persecuted, but not forsaken; struck down, but not destroyed.

2 Corinthians 4:8–9 NKJV

The Promises of God

You need to persevere so that when you have done the will of God, you will receive what he has promised.

Hebrews 10:36 NIV

Fulfilling the will of God for your lives is one of the most inspiring, life-giving, enriching adventures you will ever embark upon. He won't press his will on you, but he trusts that when you understand the people he has created you to be, you will choose to walk this amazing path he has set before you.

Should you choose God's will, you should know that it will take a full-out commitment from both of you. But you won't have to make your journey alone. He has promised to provide his wisdom, counsel, encouragement, insight, and everything else you might need to succeed. And when you've accomplished what you were created to do, he has promised to reward you for a job well done.

God, we want to live in the center of your will for our lives. We look to your promises to see us through to victory. Amen.

Fight the good fight for the faith; take hold of eternal life, to which you were called and have made a good confession.

1 Timothy 6:12 HCSB

Hold On!

Hold on to what you have, so that no one will take your crown.
Revelation 3:11 NIV

Marriage requires commitment and the ability to hold on during the tough times. No matter how long you've been married, you know that becoming one with another person isn't all smiles and kisses. The process is wrought with daily challenges. But too often couples give up before they experience the priceless benefits marriage provides—love, caring, intimacy, and more.

Learning to live a life of faith also has challenges. Your humanness won't much care for the ways of God. But like marriage, living in vital relationship with God is worth everything you invest in it. You just have to hold on in the hard times, cling to God's promises, and refuse to give up.

God, we are committed to our faith in you and our faith in each other. Help us to stay true to our commitment even in difficult times. Amen.

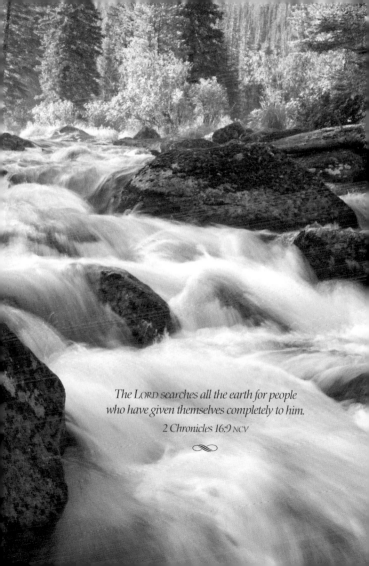

The LORD searches all the earth for people
who have given themselves completely to him.

2 Chronicles 16:9 NCV

A Matter of Trust

I know whom I have believed and I am convinced that He is able to guard what I have entrusted to Him.

2 Timothy 1:12 NASB

∽

God doesn't have trust issues. He knows what each person is capable of and what he has placed in each life. Trusting God the way he trusts you is a learning process. It is accomplished in baby steps. You trust him with something, experience his faithfulness, and then you can trust him for more. Each step takes you closer to trusting him completely.

Learning to trust God is essential. It is the key to accessing all the benefits he longs to bestow on his children. Imagine living without fear because you have learned to trust in his watchful care, and living without worry because he has promised to meet your needs.

∼

God, we want to trust you completely. Show us where to begin, and watch over us as we take our first baby steps. Amen.

The one who trusts in the
Lord will be happy.
Proverbs 16:20 HCSB

In the Race to Win

Do you not know that those who run in a race all run, but only one receives the prize? Run in such a way that you may win.

1 Corinthians 9:24 *NASB*

Yours is a living faith. God intended for you to grow in it every day, as you pursue a clear goal—to become all God created you to be and spend eternity in the presence of your creator. The Bible speaks of it as a race with a finish line and a prize.

If your walk of faith has come to a standstill, you are missing the most significant part of your lives, the part that will give you purpose and draw out your strengths and gifts. Faith will carry you through this life and beyond. Agree together to get back in the race.

God, we want back in the race. Help us to regain our stamina and keep our eyes on the prize until we reach the finish line. Amen.

I have fought well. I have finished
the race, and I have been faithful.
So a crown will be given to me
for pleasing the Lord.

2 Timothy 4:7–8 CEV

Dealing With Distractions

Stand firm and don't be shaken. Always keep busy working for the Lord. You know that everything you do for him is worthwhile.

1 Corinthians 15:58 CEV

It's a given that the minute the two of you decide to commit yourselves fully to the life of faith, distractions will begin to pop up everywhere. Your determination and endurance will be tested in ways you never thought possible. Don't be discouraged. All pilgrims of faith encounter mental struggles with being tested.

When you decide to go on a diet, thoughts of food fill your head. This passes after a short while, but if you let them, these thoughts can derail you. The same thing happens when you begin your race of faith. Don't be moved by distractions. Stay the course, and don't let anything keep you from your prize.

God, help us to deal with distractions and stay in the race. We want to please you as we go forward in our faith. Amen.

As you therefore have received Christ Jesus the Lord, continue to live your lives in him, rooted and built up in him and established in the faith.

Colossians 2:6–7 NRSV

Rewarding Determination

Be strong and do not give up, for your work will be rewarded.

2 Chronicles 15:7 NIV

∞

God created you. He knows the gifts and talents he placed in you and the dreams he wrote on your hearts. His great desire is for you to develop and use your gifts and achieve your dreams so that you can reach your full potential and become the people he created you to be.

God also understands that human beings are often weak and prone to give up easily. For this reason, he rewards your determined efforts with a strong personal sense of joy and satisfaction. He pours out his peace and his favor as well. Don't give up on the people God has called you to be. Stay the course, and reap the rewards.

God, we thank you for motivating us to fulfill our destiny and make our lives count. Amen.

Two are better than one, because they have a
good reward for their toil.

Ecclesiastes 4:9 NRSV

With All That Is Within Us

Because the Sovereign LORD helps me, I will not be disgraced. Therefore have I set my face like flint, and I know I will not be put to shame.

Isaiah 50:7 NIV

∞

Living a life of faith is the greatest thing you can do with your lives, but that doesn't mean it's easy. The road ahead is littered with obstacles and distractions. You might even be tempted to give up. This little secret will help you stay the course.

Make a formal declaration between the two of you to give this faith business everything you've got with no holding back. Put it into writing, read it to each other, and sign it. When you got married, your wedding ceremony formalized your commitment to each other, and this purposeful declaration will do the same for your faith. It will strengthen your resolve and remind you of your goal.

∞

God, we have determined to go forward
on the path of faith with everything
that is within us. Amen.

You, Lord, are a shield around me, my glory,
and the One who lifts up my head.

Psalm 3:3 HCSB

The Crown of Life

God blesses those who patiently endure testing and temptation. Afterward they will receive the crown of life that God has promised to those who love him.

James 1:12 NLT

∞

The earthly reward for living your faith is an abiding sense of significance and satisfaction. You might think that's quite enough, but there is also a reward in heaven. God has promised that those who endure testing, overcome distractions, and continue to grow in their faith will be given the crown of life.

What that will look like and how it will be worn are mysteries that will not be revealed until the day you stand before his throne and receive it from his hand. But you can be sure that it will be more amazing than anything you've ever seen before. It will identify the two of you as those who have overcome in life.

God, your rewards are extravagantly generous. We know that with you we will always receive more than we give. Amen.

I have chosen to be faithful; I have determined to live by your regulations.

Psalm 119:30 NLT

Endure to the End

We can rejoice ... when we run into problems and trials, for we know that they help us develop endurance.

Romans 5:3 NLT

Some days nothing seems to go right. One little disaster is followed by another and then another. You might even look at each other on those days and wish you hadn't even gotten up. Everyone has those days, and everyone has days when the weight of one gigantic trial or problem comes crashing down.

Great or small, you simply can't afford to let trials knock you down. Stop what you're doing and take a deep breath. Then, when you have time alone together, take hands and pray for each other. Ask God to take the brokenness of your day and put it to productive use. Then thank him for doing it.

God, we admit that we are easily defeated.
Teach us patience and fortitude. Amen.

*Every child of God can defeat the world,
and our faith is what gives us this victory.*

1 John 5:4 CEV

Being Made New

We do not give up. Our physical body is becoming older and weaker, but our spirit inside us is made new every day.

2 Corinthians 4:16 NCV

Walk for a few miles and your bodies will feel it. But walking with God has the opposite effect. Each day your spirits are emboldened, your souls are refreshed, and your minds are renewed. While your earthly bodies grow older and more tired, your spirits take on newness of life daily.

Take care of your earthly bodies. They are God's gifts, meant to serve you for this life. But know that someday you will simply slough off your old, used-up bodies, and the glowing, vibrant persons you have become inside will take on garments fit for God's royal throne room. That is the essence of God's glorious promise of eternal life.

God, when we feel the signs of aging in our bodies, we will thank you for the new bodies that will one day be ours. Amen.

We're waiting the arrival of the Savior, the Master, Jesus Christ, who will transform our earthly bodies into glorious bodies like his own.

Philippians 3:20–21 MSG

Refuse to Be Quitters

Now that we're on the right track, let's stay on it.
Philippians 3:16 MSG

The life of faith requires endurance, commitment, and the desire to win. These challenges build confidence and character. They were designed by God to take you from wimps to highly trained knights in God's kingdom. You are training on a hostile track, but God is personally overseeing your progress.

There is only one way you can lose this race for your faith—quit! Don't allow anyone to slow you down or talk you off the track. As long as you stay the course, your victory is certain. Many others have successfully run the race before you. Some of them are recognized by name in the Bible. That's how proud God is of their achievements.

God, we are ready to tie on our running shoes and set off together. We trust that you will run with us until we reach the finish line. Amen.

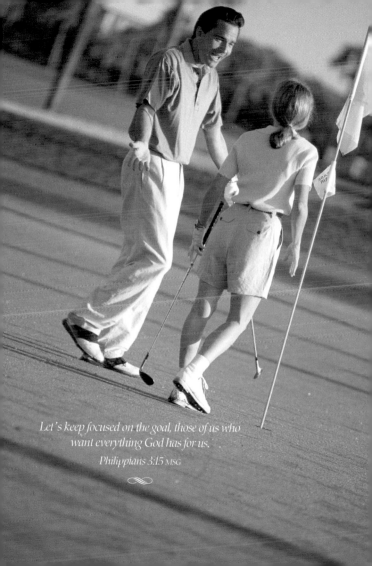

*Let's keep focused on the goal, those of us who
want everything God has for us.*

Philippians 3:15 MSG

Buoyed by Prayer

Don't burn out; keep yourselves fueled and aflame. Be alert servants of the Master, cheerfully expectant. Don't quit in hard times; pray all the harder.

Romans 12:11–12 MSG

∞

Prayer is essential to a solid relationship with God. How well would athletes do, how much could they achieve without constant dialogue with the coach? God, through his Holy Spirit, is your coach. He will provide you with encouragement, instruction, and inspiration. And he will be constantly looking out for your interests as well.

Don't hesitate to tell your coach what you need, and be quick to do what he asks of you. After all, his goal is victory in your life. If you listen to him, he can help you avoid burnout and stay motivated to accomplish great things. Like good teammates, pray together, and share the lessons you learn with each other. Work together for that big win!

God, we thank you for coaching us through
the great race of our lives. Challenge us
to reach our full potential. Amen.

Get down on your knees before the Master;
it's the only way you'll get on your feet.

James 4:10 MSG

Perspective

❧

The LORD says: "My thoughts and
my ways are not like yours."

Isaiah 55:8 CEV

The Heart Matters

What were your first impressions of each other? Was it love at first sight, or did love come later? Either way, you probably remember what you thought about each other the first time you met!

With God, there's no such thing as a first impression, because he knew you even before you were born. He's not looking at your outward appearance—how tall you are or how you dress. He knows what's in your hearts.

God not only knows your hearts, he wants you to know his. When you spend time in prayer and reading the Bible, you will come to know and understand him better. Then you will begin to see what really matters to him.

God, we want to know your heart just
as you know ours. Give us insight
and understanding as we seek to find
what really matters to you. Amen.

God does not judge by external appearance.
Galatians 2:6 NIV

Through Other Eyes

Look up, and be alert to what is going on around Christ—that's where the action is. See things from his perspective.

Colossians 3:2 MSG

As you grow together in marriage, you become increasingly familiar with each other's thoughts and feelings. You discover each other's likes and dislikes, and you discover how each other views the world. As a result, you understand each other's actions and reactions better than you did. The clearer your perspective, the better your union will be overall.

In the same way, when you read the Bible and pray, you become increasingly familiar with God's thoughts and feelings. You begin to understand better who he is and what he expects from you. This added perspective will lead to a better relationship with God.

In both your marriage and your faith, the more you know, the better you understand.

God, help us understand your will and your way with us. We desire to see each other and the world through your eyes. Amen.

As heaven is higher than earth, so My ways are higher than your ways, and My thoughts than your thoughts.

Isaiah 55:9 HCSB

Renewing Your Thoughts

Let the Spirit renew your thoughts and attitudes.

Ephesians 4:23 NLT

Whether it's a two-week vacation or only a weekend away together, it feels good to return home renewed and energized. Rested in body and mind, you're ready to tackle the routines of your day with fresh enthusiasm and ideas. Those periods of renewal are essential to your health.

Renewing your soul is equally as important. That happens as you allow the Holy Spirit to carry the emotional weight of your troubles and renew your perspective. After all, that's why God sent his Spirit to you, to establish rest, renewal, and spiritual refreshment from within.

Determine together that your thoughts will drag you down. Instead, look to God's Spirit to lift you up.

God, what a miracle it is that the Holy Spirit dwells within us. We receive with thanksgiving the rest and renewal that comes from your Spirit. Amen.

*I will give them singleness of heart
and put a new spirit within them.
I will take away their stony,
stubborn heart and give them
a tender, responsive heart.*

Ezekiel 11:19 NLT

Searching Your Hearts

The LORD searches every heart and understands every motive behind the thoughts.

1 Chronicles 28:9 NIV

∞

When outward action and inner purpose do not match, it's called *hypocrisy*. Hypocrisy, however, can lie undetected by others because no one but God can search the heart and observe the true motives behind someone's words and actions.

God searches your hearts not to scare you into obedience, but to encourage you to live freely and authentically with each other and those you encounter. His searching gaze compels you to confront inconsistencies that may lurk between your outward actions and your inner purposes. Ask him to help you think, act, and speak in sincerity and love

Let God search your hearts for the sake of your love for each other and for him.

∞

Search our hearts, God, and let our motives
match our thoughts, words, and actions
in truth and purity. Amen.

*I will remove your heart of stone
and give you a heart of flesh.*

Ezekiel 36:26 HCSB

A New Attitude

Don't be selfish; don't try to impress others. Be humble, thinking of others as better than yourselves.

Philippians 2:3 NLT

Magazines, television programs, and movies tend to give you the impression that marriage is mostly about getting what you need for yourself. But the Bible says just the opposite.

God urges you to bring an attitude of humility into your relationship, treating each other with consideration and respect and being willing to put the happiness of the other ahead of your own. Looking out for yourself first will serve to isolate you. But putting the other first will draw you closer and keep you both satisfied.

From the world's perspective, God's way is upside down. But make it your new attitude, and you will find your love for each other growing stronger and more dynamic.

God, enable us to serve each other in humility and love, understanding that in giving we receive what we need. Amen.

With God are wisdom and strength;
he has counsel and understanding.

Job 12:13 NRSV

Staying Power

You cannot point to spiritual things in the same way you can point to physical objects, yet God says spiritual things are worth much more and will outlast anything you can see, touch, or feel.

When God asks the two of you to put your trust in what you cannot see, he wants you to look beyond passing attractions and superficial appearances in order to perceive such spiritual qualities as faith, kindness, compassion, caring, and love. These spiritual qualities will be evident long after the trappings of this world have disappeared.

When you put your eyes on those things with staying power and spiritual value, you can glimpse eternity.

God, enable us to find our treasure in the spiritual and eternal rather than in the superficial and temporary. Amen.

By faith we understand that the worlds were prepared by the word of God, so that what is seen was made from things that are not visible.

Hebrews 11:3 NRSV

Two Kinds of Peace

[Jesus answered,] "Peace I leave with you; my peace I give to you. I do not give to you as the world gives. Do not let your hearts be troubled, and do not let them be afraid."

John 14:27 NRSV

Most people describe peace as the absence of war, which is the kind of peace that hangs on truces, treaties, and agreements, and is, as it has been throughout history, tentative and short-lived.

Jesus promised you peace. This peace is not necessarily a lack of conflict, but rather hearts at rest, secure in the goodness of their God. Trouble may brew in far-off countries, in your community, or in your own home, but Jesus' peace keeps you from despair and hopelessness, enabling you to work for peaceful solutions with strength and confidence.

Conflicts will always be raging as long as selfishness and hatred prevail. But your hearts need not be troubled, for Jesus, the author of peace, is by your side.

God, we thank you for allowing our hearts to rest in flawless peace even when the world is experiencing constant turmoil. Amen.

*You, Lord, give true peace. You give peace to those
who depend on you, because they trust you.*

Isaiah 26:3 NCV

Informed Choices

To set the mind on the flesh is death, but to set the mind on the Spirit is life and peace.

Romans 8:6 NRSV

Perhaps you have uttered the words *If only I had known!* after realizing you made an unfortunate choice with troubling consequences. Choices and consequences are the main reason God gave you the Bible, with its timeless truths, principles, and wisdom. He means for you to use it to gain insight and perspective as you make critical choices for your lives.

God wants you to experience genuine love, joy, and peace here on earth, and live in anticipation of eternal life in heaven. He wants to help you avoid the pitfalls that could damage your relationship and scuttle your faith. Reading the Bible will help you make informed choices that will bless you and keep you strong.

God, we thank you for giving us the
Bible so we can live according to
your plan for our lives. Amen.

The law of the LORD is perfect, restoring the soul; the testimony of the LORD is sure, making wise the simple.

Psalm 19:7 NASB

A Different View

[Jesus said,] "For whoever wants to save his life will lose it, but whoever loses his life for me will find it."

Matthew 16:25 NIV

∞

Jesus set an example for us when he willingly laid down his life. He wasn't thinking of himself. He freely gave all he had. And for that, God exalted him and rewarded him with the souls of those who would believe in him.

God is calling you to the same type of sacrifice—the kind that gives all. It probably won't mean giving your life, though one day it might. Instead it means living sacrificially, putting God's will above your own. That might play out in a corporate setting or a place far from home and security. It may be fraught with difficulty, but the rewards will resound throughout eternity.

∼

God, we give you thanks and praise for
sacrificing your own life as the perfect
example for us to follow. Amen.

Be imitators of God, as dearly loved children.
Ephesians 5:1 NEB

God's Way to the Top

Whoever wants to become great among you must be your servant, and whoever wants to be first must be your slave.

Matthew 20:26–27 NIV

∞

Who's in charge at your house? If the question makes either of you feel uncomfortable, it's time for you to step back and recognize God as the center of your family.

Problems with authority and leadership happen when two people struggle with each other for God's place in their marriage and in their home. When you both recognize him as your leader and place yourselves under his authority and in service to each other, control issues will lose their punch.

Allow God to be the head of your home. Trust him to bring out the best in both of you, establish an atmosphere of peace, and give you vital perspective in how to live together in harmony.

God, ruler of our hearts and our home, grant us the privilege of serving you and living under your authority and leadership. Amen.

*Through thick and thin, keep your hearts at attention,
in adoration before Christ, your Master.*

1 Peter 3:15 MSG

Honor and Humility

Your attitude should be the same as that of Christ Jesus: Who, being in very nature God, did not consider equality with God something to be grasped.

Philippians 2:5–6 NIV

∞

If anyone was entitled to receive the highest praise, it was Jesus Christ. He was God's Son and yet he never insisted that people honor him. Instead, he humbled himself and used his divine gifts to help and heal, and freely give sight, nourishment, and life to those he encountered from day to day.

Jesus' example is a good one to follow in your marriage, as well as in all aspects of your lives. Demanding that others honor and praise you, regardless of how much you may rightfully deserve it, will only foster resentment. Instead, use your God-given gifts freely to bless others and trust God to honor and praise you as he sees fit.

God, you have shown us how to receive praise and honor through humility. Help us to make that a guiding principle in our lives. Amen.

Those who say they live in God should
live their lives as Jesus did.

1 John 2:6 NLT

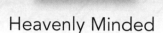

Heavenly Minded

Holy brothers and companions in a heavenly calling, consider Jesus, the apostle and high priest of our confession.

Hebrews 3:1 HCSB

It is possible for us to become so heavenly minded we're no earthly good. That might be why, when God asks us to consider spiritual matters, he points us to Jesus.

In his earthly ministry, Jesus served the needs of those he encountered. He guided them, listened to them, fed them, healed them, and even stooped to wash their feet! Jesus never degraded or ignored the troubles, sorrows, and needs of others, and Jesus remains just as caring and compassionate today.

As you set your hearts on the things of heaven, also set your hands on God's continuing work here on earth. In this way, you will nurture an "others attitude" just as Jesus did.

God, keep us faithful both in heavenly things
and in earthly things, never losing the balance
and peace we have in you. Amen.

Let each of you look not to your own interests,
but to the interests of others.

Philippians 2:4 NRSV

∞

Patience

Farmers do this all the time, waiting for their valuable crops to mature, patiently letting the rain do its slow but sure work. Be patient like that.

James 5:7 MSG

The Eyes of Love

Always be humble and gentle. Patiently put up with each other and love each other.

Ephesians 4:2 CEV

Do you remember when your best friend—the person you played with every day—grew up? Did you try to change that person, or did you accept everything—even his or her imperfections—as part of the package you knew and loved? And when you think back, which do you remember: the flaws or the fun?

Now think about each other and the commitment you've made to live together in loving harmony. Are you trying to change each other, or are you embracing the whole package? Choose not to focus on the imperfections. Instead, emphasize the good, and be patient with the rest. That's what it means to see each other through the eyes of love.

God, as you look at us through the eyes
of your love, enable us to see each
other in the same way. Amen.

A person's insight gives him patience, and his virtue is to overlook an offense.

Proverbs 19:11 HCSB

To Be Like Him

Since God chose you to be the holy people whom he loves, you must clothe yourselves with tender-hearted mercy, kindness, humility, gentleness, and patience.

Colossians 3:12 NLT

∞

Clothes make the man—or the woman. Whether or not either of you takes the adage seriously, one thing you can count on is this: God's clothes make the Christian.

You are wearing the garments God has made for you when you treat each other with attentiveness and respect both in private and in the company of others. You put on the clothing of God's Spirit when you speak highly and lovingly about each other. And you dress yourselves for success when you act with patience, compassion, and kindness even when you feel upset, hurried, or irritated.

Patience is a very special piece of God's clothing. When you wear it, your love for each other becomes stronger and more beautiful.

∞

God, clothe us both in the spiritual garments of gentleness, kindness, and patience, so we may more closely resemble you. Amen.

I will sing for joy in God! … He dressed me up in a suit of salvation, he outfitted me in a robe of righteousness.

Isaiah 61:10 MSG

Patience Comes From God

May the Lord lead your hearts into God's love and Christ's patience.
2 Thessalonians 3:5 NCV

Patience isn't part of our natural makeup. Human nature wants what it wants when it wants it. It is easily irritated and has no use for those with other ideas. It has much difficulty waiting for anyone or anything, and prefers to be first in every situation. So where does patience come from? Patience is a virtue that comes from God.

It's futile to try to become a patient person by the power of your will. Ask God to develop this characteristic in your lives. Give him permission to place you in situations where you can, with his help, overcome your natural instincts and offer others your encouragement, support, and the comfort of being themselves.

God, grant us the gift of patience with
ourselves, with those around us,
and with each other. Amen.

May the patience and encouragement that come from God allow you to live in harmony with each other the way Christ Jesus wants.

Romans 15:5 NCV

The Benefits of Patience

Patient people have great understanding.

Proverbs 14:29 NCV

Patience is an active willingness to endure the exasperations of life with wisdom, confidence, intelligence, and self-control. Patience is a virtue that grows stronger as you live in relationship with God, and it brings with it many benefits.

Did you ever have a teacher who was willing to labor with you over some difficult concept or who stood by encouragingly as you learned a new skill? You experienced the benefits of patience in that person's life. Patience offers a helping hand, provides much-needed words of encouragement, allows for second chances, and extends to you the freedom to be yourself. Patience benefits both the giver and the receiver, a characteristic common to all God's virtues.

God our Father, help us speak and act with
patience in all things so we may know
its many benefits. Amen.

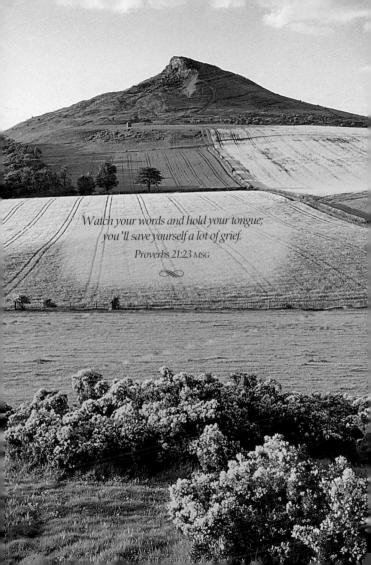

Watch your words and hold your tongue;
you'll save yourself a lot of grief.

Proverbs 21:23 MSG

Let Patience Grow

He gives strength to the weary and strengthens the powerless.

Isaiah 40:29 HCSB

∞

There is no shortcut for acquiring patience. It is the result of the Holy Spirit's working in your lives. In fact, the only way to become a patient person is practice, practice, and more practice. Of course, as you learn patience, you will face multiple challenges or opportunities to choose patience and establish it as a virtue in your lives.

Patience, like so many of God's virtues, is learned by continuing to do the right thing, not just once or twice, but again and again until it becomes embedded in your character. You no longer have to make a conscious choice because patience comes naturally to you.

∾

God, strengthen us by your Spirit as
we learn patience by walking in it
one situation at a time. Amen.

*The one who plants in response to God,
letting God's Spirit do the growth work in
him, harvests a crop of real life, eternal life.*

Galatians 6:8 MSG

Strong and Patient

Patience is better than strength.

Proverbs 16:32 NCV

∞

You've seen it happen—a powerful politician brought down because of a series of hasty and ill-advised decisions; an adored celebrity subjected to scorn due to years of impulsive, self-destructive behavior.

Similarly, two people who act without thinking, without caution, without stopping to consider the consequences of their choices, can weaken and sometimes even destroy their marriage. Conversely, two people who consistently act with patience, each stopping to reflect on how their conduct will affect the other, thinking through the likely outcome of their choices, and being willing to wait for positive and beneficial solutions to problems, can strengthen their marriage.

In all things, resolve to act with patience, because in patience lies strength.

∞

God, we thank you for your patience with us, and we pray for the strength that we need to act with consideration, care, and patience. Amen.

Be strong in the Lord and in the
power of His might.

Ephesians 6:10 NKJV

Waiting for God

I waited patiently for the
LORD. He turned to me
and heard my cry.

Psalm 40:1 NCV

The early years of your marriage can be joyous, exciting times. Then your love deepens to mature love, a love marked less by the thrill of newness and more by the closeness and warmth of mutual friendship, faithfulness, and trust.

In the same way, as you continue to grow spiritually, there may come a time when you no longer feel the excitement and enthusiasm for God you once did, and you may think God has no more to say to you. Not so! In times of God's seeming silence, his Spirit continues to move you closer to himself in the bonds of a deep and eternal relationship. Wait on God—your love for him grows deeper with time.

God, grant us the patience we need to wait
on you as you guide and direct us along
our spiritual path together. Amen.

The Lord is good to those who wait for him,
to the soul that seeks him.

Lamentations 3:25 NRSV

The Patience of Your God

Beloved, while you are waiting for these things, strive to be found by him at peace, without spot or blemish; and regard the patience of our Lord as salvation.
2 Peter 3:14–15 NRSV

∞

If you have ever doubted God's patience, just talk to someone who chose to begin a relationship with God late in life. Much of what that person has to say will reflect an awe-filled gratitude for God's constant love even after years of aimlessness and indecision.

God in his goodness deals patiently with the two of you. You are both close to his heart, and if either one of you should stumble, he will hold you, steady you, and give you the time you need to walk with him again in trust and confidence.

As God demonstrates his patience toward you, bless each other's lives with the same kind of patience. Give the gift of time.

∽

Thank you, God, for your patience with us
when we stumble. Let us give this same
patience to each other. Amen.

I wait for the LORD, my soul does wait,
and in His word do I hope.

Psalm 130:5 *NASB*

Faith and Patience

If we hope for what we do not see, we wait for it with patience.

Romans 8:25 NRSV

While couples who have been married for many years can tell you what marriage is like and perhaps offer you helpful advice, you will understand marriage best as you live it. Many dimensions of love are revealed in time spent together.

The same is true with your faith. Others might tell you how they have been blessed by their relationships with God, but faith is best understood as you walk it out. No two relationships are the same. You will come to know God in your own time and your own way as the two of you spend time together.

You can't rush faith. It is something you grow into. It's an opportunity to practice patience.

God, teach us how to wait in patience as our lives together unfold and as our hearts mature in faith and love. Amen.

*Draw near to God, and he
will draw near to you.*

James 4:8 NRSV

Waiting With Expectancy

The eyes of all look expectantly to You, and You give them their food in due season.

Psalm 145:15 NKJV

∞

Waiting is difficult when it's for something you deeply desire. If too much time passes, you may grow despondent, losing hope you will ever receive what you long for.

But there is another way to wait, no matter how intense your desire, how necessary the object of your yearnings, or how lengthy the wait turns out to be. God invites you to wait in full expectation that he knows what you are waiting for and will act on your behalf.

When? The timetable is in God's hands, as is the form his answer will take in your lives. You need only wait patiently, expecting the very best, because that is what God has in mind for you.

∞

God, we know you will give us the very best.
Help us place our complete trust in
you and your ways. Amen.

*I believe that I shall see the goodness of the
LORD in the land of the living.*

Psalm 27:13 NRSV

Troubles Don't Last Forever

God saw the trouble we were in. God's love never fails. He rescued us from our enemies.
Psalm 136:23–24 CEV

When you're going through tough times in your lives or in your marriage, or when troubles plague the lives of your loved ones, you may be tempted to think your problems will never end.

They will end, of course. Meanwhile, be patient and look to God for his help each day and as many times daily as you feel it in your heart to call on him. Talk with each other about your feelings, fears, needs, hopes, and desires, and lean on each other for support and encouragement.

Most of all look together to God to lift your burdens from your shoulders, according to his will and in his time.

God, help us lean on you for strength as we bear the rough spots in our marriage and help others in their trials. Amen.

You are my hiding place; you protect me from trouble.
You surround me with joyful shouts of deliverance.

Psalm 32:7 HCSB

Patience Is a Virtue

Staying calm settles arguments.
Proverbs 15:18 CEV
∞

What's said in a quarrel rarely stays in the quarrel; it echoes throughout the years. Angry words pierce the heart, leading to hurt feelings, reproach, and regret.

When tempers flare, patience acts like a soothing balm or a refreshing breeze. Patience refuses to respond to what is said, but it hears the distress and anguish of the other, tenderly reaching out to lift the burden, relieve the pain, ease the fear, and calm the heart. Patience never answers with reproach, but it replies in kindness and compassion.

The two of you will have disagreements—every couple does—but if you act with patience, your words will serve to heal your relationship rather than to pull it apart.

God, help us respond with patience, especially when we hear hurtful words. Teach us to be healers of the heart. Amen.

When you talk, do not say harmful things, but
say what people need—words that will help
others become stronger.

Ephesians 4:29 NCV

Patience Is the Way of Love

Love is kind and patient,
never jealous, boastful,
proud, or rude.
1 Corinthians 13:4–5 CEV

Love lies at the heart of patience. Love is one of the primary ways the two of you walk out your feelings for each other and for others.

Patience allows your loved ones to grow and never imposes its will on them. Patience encourages, guides, and celebrates small successes. Patience recognizes your loved one's limitations and does not speak sarcastically or harbor contempt. Patience bestows on those you love the gift of time—time to mature, time to surrender to God's instruction, time to learn from their actions, time to become the people God created.

Show your love by being patient with each other. It won't always be easy, but God is there to help you.

God, as you have given us the gift of love,
enable us to express it by being patient
with each other. Amen.

Those who speak with care will be rewarded.

Proverbs 18:21 *NCV*

Waiting for God

Few things are more frustrating than the feeling that the person you are speaking to is not listening. In marriage, it causes distress; in spiritual life, it lies at the root of anguish and confusion.

In the Bible, God is speaking to you. Are you listening to him tell you about his love for you, his comfort, and his compassion? Or are you too busy to hear his messages of inspiration and encouragement? Are you unwilling to hear things that might disturb or challenge you? It takes patience to listen!

When you read the Bible, you are reading God's words written out of his love for you. Be an attentive and patient listener.

God, give us patience to truly listen to
you and to each other that our lives
might be blessed. Amen.

*Those who hear the word of God
and keep it are blessed!*

Luke 11:28 HCSB

Forgiveness

Forgiveness is your habit, and that's
why you're worshiped.

Psalm 130:4 MSG

Gracious and Merciful

You are a God ready to forgive, gracious and merciful, slow to anger and abounding in steadfast love.

Nehemiah 9:17 NRSV

The words *gracious* and *merciful* are commonly used to describe God, but as you continue to walk with God and even more closely reflect his ways, *gracious* and *merciful* can also describe the two of you.

You reflect the tender grace God showers on you when you see each other through eyes of compassion, each putting the other's interests and well-being ahead of your own. You mirror the undeserved mercy God pours out on you when you're willing to forgive each other's faults because you know that God continues to forgive you.

Can you imagine the joy of marriage between two gracious and merciful people? With God's Spirit at work in your hearts, it is yours for the taking!

God, grant us hearts filled with your grace
and mercy so that others may see your
Spirit at work in us. Amen.

Since God has shown us great mercy, I beg you to offer your lives as a living sacrifice to him.

Romans 12:1 NCV

The Power of Confession

If we confess our sins to him, he is faithful and just to forgive us our sins and to cleanse us from all wickedness.
1 John 1:9 NLT

With knowledge of God's commandments and his will for your lives comes awareness of your inability to live up to his standards. Despite your best intentions, you will miss the mark.

God knows this, and he has devised a remedy for it. Rather than denying your inadequacies and letting them cloud your lives with guilt, God invites you to confess them to him in complete assurance of his forgiveness.

Trying to live perfectly on your own will only lead to frustration and failure. Ask God to guide you away from temptation and help you to make godly choices. Then thank him for his mercy and forgiveness when you fall short.

God, forgive the sins we have committed against you, and give us the grace to confess our faults to each another. Amen.

The one who conceals his sins will not prosper, but whoever confesses and renounces them will find mercy.

Proverbs 28:11 HCSB

It Is Done!

I forgive you all that you have done, says the Lord God.

Ezekiel 16:63 NRSV

Perhaps you have sought God's forgiveness, but you feel one particular wrong is too serious or shameful to be forgiven. Let it go. God has made it clear in the Bible that he is willing and able to forgive all wrongdoing, even those transgressions you may deem unforgivable.

Kneel before him with a repentant heart, confess the thing that is clutching at your conscience, and let him release you from its grip. Guilt is like a rotten apple. It will spoil everything it touches, including your marriage.

Though you may have to deal with the earthly consequences of your wrongdoing, God says your eternal soul has been cleansed and made new.

God, free us from the bonds of our human transgressions and give us the grace to both forgive and be forgiven. Amen.

Jesus said to her, "Neither do I
condemn you; go and sin no more."

John 8:11 NKJV

Free at Last

*The LORD sets
prisoners free.
Psalm 146:7 CEV*

∞

A prisoner stepping outside the gates of the prison might speak these words: "It's hard to believe I'm free at last!" What happiness must fill that human heart just to be able to walk down the street and carry on a normal life!

As both of you experience God's forgiveness, the same kind of joy will sweep over your hearts. God's forgiveness means you are no longer confined by the bonds of guilt or forced to sit in the shadows of self-reproach. Instead, you are free at last to walk with God and with each other in confidence, joy, and security. Thank God for forgiveness, for in his pardon, you are free at last!

∼

God, we thank and praise you for your
great goodness to us by freeing us
from the bonds of sin. Amen.

Blessed is the man whose sin the Lord will never count against him.

Romans 4:8 NIV

Far, Far Away!

As far as the east is from the west, so far has [God] removed our transgressions from us.

Psalm 103:12 NKJV

Throughout the Bible, God proclaims his readiness to forgive, no matter what you may have done wrong. He wants his people to place full confidence in the forgiveness won by Jesus on the cross.

When your faith rests in Jesus' triumph over death, your past mistakes have no power to shadow you or your marriage with ongoing guilt, accusations, or recriminations. You are not identified by God as a pair of wrongdoers but as his children, cleansed and free. Through Jesus, God has changed all the rules!

Though your mistakes may have brought untold suffering into your lives and your relationship, God's forgiveness puts its guilt far away from you.

God, turn us to Jesus so that we might
live in the sunshine of forgiveness
and transformed lives. Amen.

He has delivered us from the power of darkness and
conveyed us into the kingdom of the Son of His love.

Colossians 1:13 NKJV

Following His Example

Be kind and merciful, and forgive others, just as God forgave you because of Christ.

Ephesians 4:32 CEV

∞

During his walk on earth, Jesus, true man and true God, resisted temptation, prayed for others, and forgave all those who rose up against him. This is the example that God invites the two of you to follow as you walk with each other in marriage.

God realizes you will fall short of Jesus' example. After all, Jesus lived in perfect accord with God's will, which is impossible for any of his earthly children. You can, however, look to him for guidance and direction, and commit yourselves to follow his example of goodness, compassion, and forgiveness.

With humble hearts, follow him by living in constant forgiveness, never allowing the stain of bitterness to leave its trace on your lives.

∽

God, as we look to you as an example of
how to live, teach us how to abide in
an attitude of forgiveness. Amen.

In Christ, God was reconciling the world to Himself,
not counting their trespasses against them, and He
has committed the message of reconciliation to us.

2 Corinthians 5:19 HCSB

Releasing Others

*If you forgive anyone,
I also forgive him. And
what I have forgiven—if
there was anything to
forgive—I have forgiven
in the sight of Christ
for your sake.*

2 Corinthians 2:10 NIV

∾

You say "No problem" in response to a hurtful remark or action, but in your heart, there is a problem. Even though you want to mean it, you're hurt, and you resent letting the offender off so easily.

At those times, God's Spirit will remind you of the occasions God has forgiven you simply because you offered a tearfully spoken apology. He will help you recall the times he lifted your guilt because you were sincerely sorry. God does not resent letting you off so easily. Instead, he rejoices in bringing you back to him so quickly.

When you're hurt, offer your forgiveness freely. Release each other just as easily as God releases you.

⌒

God, enable us through your Spirit not only
to forgive freely but also to release
each other from guilt. Amen.

No condemnation now exists for those in Christ Jesus.

Romans 8:1 HCSB

The Responsibility of Forgiveness

Whenever you stand praying, forgive, if you have anything against anyone, so that your Father who is in heaven will also forgive you your transgressions.

Mark 11:25 NASB

∞

Imagine seeing a wealthy person refusing to offer even a dime to someone in need. Wouldn't you shake your heads in disbelief? Yet when you ask God to forgive your transgressions without being willing to forgive each other's offenses, you are in league with that wealthy person.

Of course, some offenses may be virtually unforgivable by human standards. So how could God expect you to forgive the unforgivable? You should know that forgiveness is a decision, a surrendering of the offense and offender to God's justice. This action releases you from the destructive nature of hatred and bitterness. As God helps you, the feelings associated with forgiveness will follow over time.

God, bring us to a full realization of the responsibility we have to forgive others as willingly as you forgive us. Amen.

Confess your sins to each other
and pray for each other.

James 5:16 NCV

The Work of the Heart

*Do not judge, and you
will not be judged; do
not condemn, and you
will not be condemned.
Forgive, and you will
be forgiven.*

Luke 6:37 NRSV

∞

Many long-married couples finish each other's sentences and know what is going to be said before the words are spoken. Unfortunately, the delight of knowing each other so well is often linked to the presumption you can actually see the other's motivations and intentions—the matters of the heart.

Over time, you may become certain of each other's character, disposition, and dreams. But only God sees the depths of your hearts. Only he knows your true motivations. Therefore, he rightly warns that you should not be judging each other. Determine to give each other the benefit of the doubt and leave the rest to God. Let him be the one who deals with your hearts.

∞

God, as our love deepens, we determine not to judge each other but to leave the work of the heart in your hands. Amen.

I, the LORD, examine the
mind, I test the heart.

Jeremiah 17:10 HCSB

Without Offense

Give to everyone who asks you, and if anyone takes what belongs to you, do not demand it back. Do to others as you would have them do to you.

Luke 6:30–31 NIV

In every marriage, there's give and take. Offense arises, however, when one of you begins to feel that you are doing all the giving without getting enough back.

While God doesn't want you to take advantage of each other, he does ask each of you to give freely without keeping score and without expecting anything in return. God invites you to become a genuine giver—one who harbors no resentment if the other fails to give in kind.

What you do for each other should be done gladly out of love. Where goodness and love are doing the giving, where they are the only motive, no offense is meant or taken.

God, keep us willing to be the giver in our marriage, and as we receive from each other, let us receive with thanksgiving. Amen.

*Whatever you want others to do
for you, do also the same for them.*

Matthew 7:12 HCSB

Doing the Right Thing

If you forgive others for the wrongs they do to you, your Father in heaven will forgive you.

Matthew 6:14 CEV

When you forgive, you're doing the right thing for others and for yourself.

By forgiving others completely and without fail, you free yourself from anger, bitterness, and resentment—emotions with the power to burden your heart and take away your joy in living. In addition, when you refuse to look for an opportunity to get back at someone who wronged you, people notice. You earn their admiration and respect. And in being a forgiving person yourself, you make it difficult for others to withhold forgiveness from you!

When you readily and willingly forgive each other, you're doing the right thing for both of you. You are freeing each other to grow and prosper.

God, enable us do the right thing for our marriage and for ourselves by committing ourselves to forgive each other. Amen.

Peter . . . asked, "Master, how many times
do I forgive a brother or sister who hurts me?
Seven?" Jesus replied, "Seven! Hardly.
Try seventy times seven."

Matthew 18:21–22 MSG

Fresh Start

If you've experienced a rough patch in your marriage, you may want to make a fresh start in hopes of reclaiming the love and happiness you once shared. This is an honorable choice, but to be successful, you will need to take some important steps.

First, truly forgive and be forgiven, relinquishing your various offenses to God. Second, agree not to revisit the past. Some couples just sweep the past under the carpet. Instead, you should sweep it out the door and out of your lives. Third, don't indulge guilt. Fourth, make a formal renewal of your commitment to each another. Include God, and ask him to change your hearts so you won't make the same mistakes again.

God, we ask you to help us make a fresh start.
Enable us to forgive, put the past behind us,
and move forward with our lives. Amen.

You have begun to live the new life, in which
you are being made new and are becoming
like the One who made you

Colossians 3:10 NCV

Bringing to Remembrance

Put up with each other,
and forgive anyone who
does you wrong, just as
Christ has forgiven you.

Colossians 3:13 CEV

The comment "How quickly we forget!" is often made in jest, but it applies in all seriousness to the hurts and offenses couples often bring on each other.

You may have little trouble recalling the offenses committed against you, but you may easily forget the times you committed equal, if not greater, offenses against others. Try it and see. What do you remember more vividly: offenses by you, or offenses against you? If the latter, you may be breeding more pride than humility.

When you feel you have been offended, quickly remember your own hurtful words and actions, and then forgive each other. Go out of your way to give as good as you get—as long as that's love and forgiveness.

God, grant that the remembrance of our
own sins may compel us to forgive and
forget the sins of others. Amen.

My sins you let go of, threw them over your shoulder—good riddance!

Isaiah 38:17 MSG

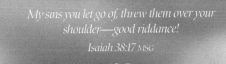

Forgiveness Brings Healing

He sent His word and healed them, and delivered them from their destructions.

Psalm 107:20 NKJV

∞

Forgiveness is like a soothing balm, a salve you might apply to an open wound. As you spread salve on a physical injury, the swelling goes down, redness fades, heat dissipates, and the wound is protected from infection.

When you have a spiritual wound, God offers you forgiveness to calm the ache and heal your broken heart. The soothing balm of forgiveness provides solace and strength to begin the healing process and protect you from the infection of bitterness and anger.

Together take your spiritual wounds to God. Bow before him, and allow him to bring healing to your souls. There is no reason for suffering to continue when God is present.

∼

God, apply the healing balm of forgiveness
to our wounds and allow us to grow
in spiritual strength. Amen.

"I will restore you to health and I will heal you of your wounds," declares the LORD.

Jeremiah 30:17 NASB

The Time to Forgive Is Now

There's an opportune time to do things, a right time for everything on the earth.... A right time to hold on and another to let go.

Ecclesiastes 3:1, 6 MSG

∞

If you have ever missed a once-in-a-lifetime opportunity because you failed to act quickly enough, you realize that life doesn't always offer a second chance.

You can never assume there will be a next time to ask someone you have offended for forgiveness, another more convenient time to express your regret, or a later time to say what needs to be said. Equally, you can never assume there will be another chance to hear the healing words of reconciliation from someone moved by your sincerity and sorrow.

In all your relationships, and most especially in your marriage, the time to forgive is now, and the time to extend your hand in reconciliation and peace is now.

∽

God, let us never delay to confess our wrongs to each other, and never wait to extend our hands in reconciliation and peace. Amen.

God has planned a time for every thing and every action.

Ecclesiastes 3:17 NCV

Love Has Broad Shoulders

*Love overlooks the
wrongs that others do.*

Proverbs 10:12 CEV

∞

As long as you're living on this side of heaven, your mistakes and those of others will affect and infect your lives. At some time, you will be hurt, saddened, confused, and angry because someone did or said the wrong thing. And at some other time, you will be the one doing or saying the wrong thing.

God promises that love overpowers mistakes. For as much chaos as mistakes may cause, he says love can ease their effects, deflect their pain, and find the good in every bad situation. Love rushes to cover those mistakes, even smother them, by motivating you to respond with kindness, forgiveness, compassion, caring, wisdom, and understanding. Love is strong and has broad shoulders.

God, grant us the Spirit-fed faith we need
to meet our challenges and cover our
griefs with the power of love. Amen.

*The steadfast love of the L*ORD *never ceases,*
his mercies never come to an end;
they are new every morning.

Lamentations 3:22–23 NRSV

Guarding Your Forgiven Hearts

Whatever is true, whatever is noble, whatever is right, whatever is pure, whatever is lovely, whatever is admirable— if anything is excellent or praiseworthy—think about such things.

Philippians 4:8 NIV

Whenever there's a vacuum, something rushes in to fill it. In a cleansed, forgiven, and renewed human heart, emptied of bitterness and rage, there is a vacuum waiting to be filled.

If you leave your hearts unguarded, old thoughts and habits return. When they do, you have not only your old lives back, but the added burden of admitting you have failed to live up to your best intentions. Ask God's Spirit to enter your hearts and gladden them with new thoughts and habits. Delight in God-pleasing ideas, and fill your lives with God-pleasing activities and relationships.

Guard your cleansed and forgiven hearts that they might be filled with all the goodness of God.

God, leave no room in our hearts for unholy thoughts, but fill our hearts and lives with all things pleasing to you. Amen.

*We use our powerful God-tools . . . fitting
every loose thought and emotion and impulse
into the structure of life shaped by Christ.*

2 Corinthians 10:5 MSG

Peace at Last

The wonderful thing about forgiveness is the peace it brings in its wake. It can be difficult to forgive, but with it comes resolution and calm!

Close your eyes for a moment and remember the last time someone offended you. You probably remember the turmoil, the anger, and the indignation. Maybe you couldn't sleep. You suffered. Now remember how it felt when you forgave that offense. Though it was painful, the act of forgiveness probably calmed you and allowed you to rest. It brought you peace.

The question is, how long did you suffer unnecessarily before you were able to forgive? Resolve together that you will choose the peace of forgiveness and bask in its healing power.

God, grant us hearts at peace with you and with each other, and give us all the blessing that comes from forgiveness. Amen.

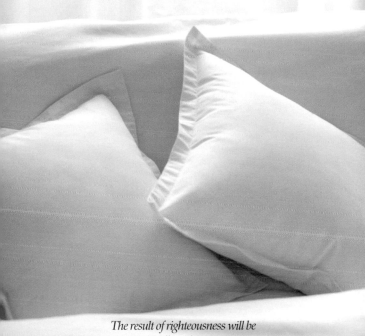

The result of righteousness will be peace; the effect of righteousness will be quiet confidence forever.

Isaiah 32:17 HCSB

Joy

❧

The LORD's instruction is right; it makes
our hearts glad. His commands shine
brightly, and they give us light.

Psalm 19:8 CEV

The Joy of Pleasing God

For the one who pleases him God gives wisdom and knowledge and joy.

Ecclesiastes 2:26 NRSV

God wants you to please him. In fact, he insists on it. But wait a minute—isn't he supposed to be selfless and humble? Seems like he wants to be the center of attention, doesn't it?

On the surface, it does sound like God is stuck on himself, some egotistical king on his throne. But consider this. When you were a child you pleased your parents by obeying their rules (which kept you safe) and getting good grades (an investment in your future). Ultimately, pleasing them meant doing those things that were in your best interest. Joy comes when you realize that pleasing God is all about the selflessness of a father's love.

God in heaven, we want to know the joy
of pleasing you. Thank you for looking
after our best interests. Amen.

*We ... do not cease to pray for
you ... that you may walk worthy of
the Lord, fully pleasing Him.*

Colossians 1:9–10 NKJV

The Joy of God's Blessings

The LORD your God will bless you in all your produce and in all the work of your hands, so that you surely rejoice.

Deuteronomy 16:15 NKJV

You have to admit, God is well known for his blessings. No one knows how to bless you quite as well as he does, and for a reason. God doesn't stumble over himself trying to decide what would make you truly happy because he already knows. He created you. He knows you inside and out.

God is a master at bringing joy to the hearts of those who are willing to reach out and taste of his goodness. But his blessings often bypass those things you may think you want and provide instead those things you really need. God's blessings are wrapped in joy because they aren't superficial. They are real and lasting and represent God's best for you.

God, your blessings bring us great joy.
Thank you for providing what we need
on all the levels of our lives. Amen.

See if I will not open the windows of heaven
for you and pour down for you an overflowing
blessing ... says the LORD of hosts.

Malachi 3:10 NRSV

Joyful Souls

Why are you here? What is the purpose of your existence? Human beings have been asking those questions for thousands of years. Maybe the two of you have wondered as well.

Because the mind tends to complicate things, most people overlook the simple answer. Your purpose is to please God, to shine before your Creator, to live the fullness of life he planned for you. Once you understand that truth, everything changes. You stop struggling to be what others want you to be and focus on becoming the real you, the persons you were born to be.

Living authentically releases your inner joy, and nothing compares to that. It is a joy that comes from relishing every moment of life.

∾

God, we thank you for restoring to us the joy
of living, and for revealing to us the
purpose for our lives. Amen.

We ask God to accept us.
Then we joyfully worship God.

Job 33:26 <small>CEV</small>

Joyful Lips

The mouth speaks out of that which fills the heart.

Matthew 12:34 NASB

When the Bible speaks about the heart, it doesn't mean the organ that circulates blood; the Bible is talking about the soul, the innermost self. The soul is often referred to metaphorically as the heart because it operates in much the same way. Instead of circulating blood through the body, the soul disburses whatever has been stored inside it.

The heart is filled with good things like love, peace, courage, and hope, which bring a smile to the face, health to the body, and a song on the lips. If you long for real, lasting joy in your lives, ask God to clean you up on the inside. Banish negativity, and encourage hope and love to grow in your hearts.

God, we want to bless ourselves and others
with the joy that comes from knowing
good things fill our hearts. Amen.

[God] will yet fill your mouth with laughter
and your lips with shouts of joy.

Job 8:21 NIV

Joyous Truth

The word of the LORD is right, and all His work is done in truth.

Psalm 33:4 NKJV

Joy and happiness are not the same thing. Happiness comes and goes with your circumstances. Sure, it's wonderful while it lasts, but it could be gone in an instant.

Joy, on the other hand, resonates from deep inside as a response to the touch of God. It doesn't fluctuate with external circumstances. Rather, it strengthens you at your core. Joy is a response to certain truths that are unchanging. One such truth is that God loves you. Another is that his forgiveness covers you completely. Still another is that he has endowed you with specific gifts and talents with which to bless yourselves and others. And yet another is that your future is secure in his hands.

Dear God, we thank you for the joy that comes with recognizing the truth of your presence in our lives. Amen.

What you're after is truth from the inside out.
Enter me, then; conceive a new, true life.

Psalm 51:6 MSG

Joyful Attitudes

A friendly smile makes you happy.
Proverbs 15:30 CEV

You know how it feels to be in a bad mood, and then someone walks in and starts clowning around. Maybe you resist at first, but finally you are helpless to stop what you know is coming. You break out in a smile, and the bad mood vanishes.

No one is in a good mood all the time—that's just not human. But keeping a good mental attitude can make a measurable difference. When you feel yourself slipping out of the positive into the negative, remind yourself of all the things you have to be grateful for. Count your blessings with each other until the joy that resides in your hearts wells up and spills over, chasing that sour mood away.

God, we thank you for the blessings you have poured out on our lives. Just remembering them fills us with joy. Amen.

Happiness makes you smile.

Proverbs 15:13 CEV

Watching God at Work

The humble will see their God at work and be glad. Let all who seek God's help be encouraged.

Psalm 69:32 NLT

Picture yourself holding a raffle ticket, waiting to see if your three-digit number will be called. You hold your breath with expectation, and then you hear the first number. It matches. The second number is called. It too matches. A cloud of excitement builds around your head, and then the third number is called. Win or lose, waiting like this for good luck to happen fails more often than it succeeds.

Trusting God, however, is a sure thing. When you place your expectation in him, he goes to work on your behalf. And when he's through, you have more than a worthless raffle ticket to show for it. God's help won't always come in the form you expect, but it always comes, and, oh, what joy it brings with it.

God, we bring our needs to you, because you are always working on our behalf. Your willingness to help us fills our hearts with joy. Amen.

*My help comes from the L*ORD,
who made heaven and earth.

Psalm 121:2 NKJV

Deep, Renewing Joy

Light is shed upon the righteous and joy on the upright in heart.

Psalm 97:11 NIV

In spite of the fact that there are multiplied trillions of stars in space, too many to count, in fact, astronomers say there is astonishing order to it all. A natural harmony points to its Creator. You are God's creation as well, designed to fulfill a grand and noble purpose in this life. That's why joy comes when you live as God intended.

Your accomplishments in this life, and whatever fame or fortune you might win, may bring you happiness. But that happiness cannot compare to the deep, renewing joy that floods your lives when your hearts are right with God and you are walking in his purpose and design.

God, we desire to live in harmony with your grand design for our lives. Show us how to do that one joy-filled day at a time. Amen.

*Clothe yourselves with the new self, created
according to the likeness of God in true
righteousness and holiness.*

Ephesians 4:24 NRSV

Singing With Joy

Shout joyfully to the LORD, all the earth. Serve the LORD with gladness; come before Him with joyful singing.

Psalm 100:1–2 NASB

Living in harmony with your Creator, as you may have already learned, graces your life with a deep joy that longs to be expressed. Common manifestations are smiling, shouting, singing, even dancing. If you should feel this joy rising up within you, don't hold back.

Wave your arms in the air, clap your hands, move from side to side, and give your lips permission to describe—as best they can—all that is in your hearts. When the burst of joy subsides, you'll find that you are calmer, more relaxed, and in a better mood. Your health, body and soul, will be enhanced and strengthened.

God, your presence in our lives brings us great joy. Thank you for the ability to express that joy. Amen.

The joy of the Lord will make you strong.

Nehemiah 8:10 NCV

Rejoice in God's Laws

*Your statutes are my
heritage forever, O LORD,
they are the joy
of my heart.*
Psalm 119:111 NIV

∞

Laws of any kind are often considered the opposite of freedom; negatives restricting certain actions. But most laws are actually intended for personal and corporate good. Without them, life would be chaotic and dangerous.

The same is true for God's laws. Some people dismiss them as old-fashioned constructs that keep people from enjoying their lives. But just like human laws, God's laws are intended to keep you from wandering off and losing your way. They keep you on the path to fullness of life and fulfillment of purpose. They restrict a different kind of freedom, the freedom to waste opportunities, make poor choices, and wander into harm's way. Rejoice in God's laws. They are the keys to a good life.

God, we honor and rejoice in your laws because
we understand that they are intended to
free us to live joyful lives. Amen.

Happy are those who keep the law.

Proverbs 29.18 NRSV

Joyous Thanks

*The LORD has done
amazing things for us!
What joy!*

Psalm 126:3 NLT

Can you remember a Christmas or birthday when you asked for something special and received it? What was your response? Did you just sit there and smile or did you jump around the room saying "Thank you, thank you, thank you" at the top of your lungs?

Take some time to remember the good things God has brought to your lives. You won't be able to name them all, because God often does amazing things for you that you don't even know about. Just naming the obvious, however, will inspire thankfulness and joy. Thank him for the amazing things you don't see, and your heart will rejoice even more.

God, we thank you for all you have done for us. You have given us the desire of our hearts and reasons to shout for joy. Amen.

With great joy, you people will get water from
the well of victory. At that time you will say,
"Our Lord, we are thankful."

Isaiah 12:3–4 CEV

The Fullness of Joy

Ask and you will receive, so that your joy will be the fullest possible joy.

John 16:24 NCV

Do you know what God desires for you? He wants you to lead good, productive, satisfying, fulfilled, joyous lives, never missing even one good thing. He wants your cup of joy to be full to the brim.

For that reason, he invites you to go to him and ask for what you need. Of course, he could just shower his gifts and blessings down on you, and he often does. But other times it is important for you to ask. That way you know that he hears you and answers. Take all your requests to God and let him demonstrate how much he loves you. There is great joy in knowing you are loved.

God, we thank you for hearing us when we pray and blessing us with your answers. It brings us joy to know you are looking after us. Amen.

Your good people should celebrate and shout.

Psalm 32:11 CEV

Celebrating the Joy Giver

*Celebrate God all day,
every day. I mean,
revel in him!*

Philippians 4:4 MSG

∞

You've probably heard God called the Creator or the Judge, but have you ever heard him called the Joy Giver? And yet he is the one, the only one, who can bring lasting joy to your lives. He gives your existence meaning, showers you with blessings, and sticks by you in good times and bad.

Let your voices rise in celebration of the One who puts music in your hearts and thanksgiving on your lips. Show him appreciation for bringing the two of you together and for the good things you enjoy every day. Once you get started celebrating the Joy Giver, you may not be able to stop, and that brings joy to God's heart.

∼

God, we are grateful for all the things you
have done for us. May our lives bring you
joy just as you bring joy to us. Amen.

*You have been good to me, L*ORD,
and I will sing about you.

Psalm 13:6 CEV

Rejoicing in the Truth

If asked, you would probably say you value truth. You want to be told the truth, and you want to be truthful with others. The reality, however, is that truth can be tough to swallow. That's why, in many cases, you may look for ways to skirt around it. That's natural; that's part of human nature. But it can cause you to miss out.

Some truth, though difficult to receive, will bring great good to your lives. One such truth, for example, is that every person has a hole in his or her heart that can be filled only by God. You need him. That truth, once embraced, will bring you the kind of joy you've never before known.

God, we rejoice in the truth that we need you in our lives. We invite you to walk with us as we make our journey through this life. Amen.

O LORD; let Your lovingkindness and
Your truth continually preserve me.

Psalm 40:11 NKJV

The Joy of Living

You will make known to me the path of life; in Your presence is fullness of joy.

Psalm 16:11 NASB

∞

If you asked people what would make them happy, you might get answers like "winning the lottery" or "marrying well" or "going on a lavish vacation." But if you asked what brings them joy, you might hear something like "my grandchildren" or "my pet" or "a romantic dinner with the one I love." The simple things bring joy to life.

Spend some time naming those things that bring you joy. Take turns identifying one joy at a time, and after each one, pause to thank God for the simple joy expressed. It might be wise to have a box of tissues handy. You will probably shed a few joyful tears.

God, we thank you for all the seemingly little things that bring such pure joy to our lives. We consider ourselves rich with blessings. Amen.

*May you enjoy the good things of Jerusalem
all your life. May you see your grandchildren.*

Psalm 128:5–6 NCV

Your Happiness Comes From God

Joyful indeed are those whose God is the LORD.

Psalm 144:15 NLT

How do you see God? Is he the ultimate authority who sits in the heavens and judges those on earth? Or an impersonal creator, who flung the stars into the sky, created humankind, and then withdrew to watch stoically from the heavens? Even believing that God doesn't exist means you've given your relationship with him some thought.

In the Bible, God extends himself to you. He has said that if you seek him, you will find him; if you knock, the door will be opened. If you haven't done so already, reach out to him. Give him the opportunity to reach back, proving his love for you. All happiness and joy are resident in knowing him.

God, we long to know you, to see you as you really are. Thank you for loving us and opening your arms wide. Amen.

I stand at the door. I knock. If you hear me call and open the door, I'll come right in and sit down to supper with you.

Revelation 3:20 MSG

Tough Times

Call upon Me in the day of trouble;
I shall rescue you, and you will honor Me.

Psalm 50:15 NASB

God Is Always There

Is anyone crying for help? God is listening, ready to rescue you.

Psalm 34:17 MSG

∞

Crisis brings with it many unsettling emotions: fear, uncertainty, isolation, self-doubt, and sometimes guilt. It can be a difficult time, and these events are typically unexpected, allowing no time for preparation and planning.

You don't have to suffer through your crises alone, however. In the Bible, God promised to see you through every adverse situation. Like a loving father, God hears your crying and empathizes with your suffering. He helps you emerge from the fog long enough to consider solutions. He isn't simply a convenient friend; you can depend on God. He is always there for you when you need him, in the good times and in the bad.

∞

God, when our hearts are saddened and our
problems seem to be swallowing us up,
we will look to you for help. Amen.

The LORD has heard my cry for help;
the LORD will answer my prayer.

Psalm 6:9 NCV

He Will Comfort You

I was very worried, but you comforted me and made me happy.
Psalm 94:19 NCV

God could have chosen any of a limitless number of characteristics to describe the Holy Spirit, his presence residing in the hearts and lives of his children, but he chooses to call him the Comforter. Just imagine—the primary task of the matchless Spirit of God is to comfort you as you pass through the trials and tribulations of this life.

You may be worried about some circumstance in your lives, or you may be afraid, lonely, confused, disappointed, angry, or disillusioned. Whatever the case, God's Holy Spirit is there to comfort you. You are never alone in your troubles. Reach out to him and rejoice in the knowledge that he is by your side.

God, we thank you for sending your Holy Spirit to extend to us your love, support, and comfort as we live out our lives here on earth. Amen.

[The Lord] takes care of his people like a
shepherd. He gathers them like lambs in his
arms and carries them close to him.

Isaiah 40:11 NCV

Your Weakness, His Grace

He said to me, "My grace is sufficient for you, for power is made perfect in weakness."

2 Corinthians 12:9 NRSV

Independence is a natural part of the human nature. Even babies demonstrate this as they learn to walk, talk, and navigate their surroundings. "I do it myself" is the catch phrase of most toddlers. This human characteristic allows growth and the ability to take responsibility in life. Too much independence, however, can lead to pride, and pride can keep you from seeking God's help when times are hard.

Pretence is lost on God. He knows you better than you know yourself. And he knows those areas where you struggle. Rather than negatives, he sees them as opportunities to demonstrate his great love and concern for you. Let him shore up your weaknesses with his great strength.

God, forgive us when we stubbornly try to deal with our troubles on our own. We thank you for being there to help us. Amen.

Depend on the L<small>ORD</small> *and his strength; always go to him for help.*

1 Chronicles 16:11 *NCV*

Overflowing Comfort

Just as the sufferings of Christ flow over into our lives, so also through Christ our comfort overflows.

2 Corinthians 1:5 NIV

Those who espouse faith in God soon find that certain trials come along with it. Some have encountered persecution, but all realize that difficult choices and changes must be made. Certain habits, mind-sets, and even relationships must be sacrificed if a person is to grow into maturity as a child of God.

You can be certain, though, that sacrifices are noticed by God. He sees, he cares, and he comforts. As you put unsavory elements of your old life behind you, he promises to replace them with an abundance of rich blessings. You cannot give more than God can. What you give up for him will be repaid many times over.

God, we ask you to show us those things that are holding us back from being the people you created us to be. Thank you for your limitless blessings. Amen.

*What we are suffering now cannot compare
with the glory that will be shown to us.*

Romans 8:18 CEV

You Are Survivors

We are hard pressed on every side, but not crushed; perplexed, but not in despair; persecuted, but not abandoned; struck down, but not destroyed.

2 Corinthians 4:8–9 NIV

Your faith in God will not change the fact that the two of you live in an imperfect world. No one lives in the sunshine all the time; everyone experiences rainy days. What you can depend on is that God will not allow your trials and tribulations to destroy you. His presence in your lives takes away fear and anxiety and allows you to address your troubles with patience, wisdom, and inner strength.

When you are walking with God, your path with its obstacles and pitfalls remains the same. The change comes inside you. No longer are you hapless victims, crushed by your circumstances. Instead, you are courageous overcomers; you are survivors.

God, we thank you for walking with us as we take our journey through life. We look to you to help us overcome. Amen.

In all these things we overwhelmingly conquer
through Him who loved us.

Romans 8:37 NASB

Never Alone

Be strong and courageous. Do not be afraid or terrified ... for the LORD your God goes with you; he will never leave you nor forsake you.

Deuteronomy 31:6 NIV

Deep within every human soul is the fear of being abandoned and alone. It is a fear common to humankind, regardless of how nurturing and present one's parents have been. Some cope by staying busy; others cope by accumulating possessions and various other forms of security. And some put their efforts into nurturing relationships so that if one fails another will be available.

Still, if we are honest, activities, riches, and human relationships do not survive this life. Only God can promise that he will never leave you nor forsake you, that he will be with you both now and forever. Only God's love can quiet your fears and provide the security you long for.

God, your promises restore our lives.
You are the key to fearless living. Thank
you for your unending love. Amen.

*I have been young, and now am old, yet I
have not seen the righteous forsaken or
their children begging bread.*

Psalm 37:25 NRSV

He Holds the Future

The vision is yet for the appointed time.

Habakkuk 2:3 HCSB

∞

The future always has been and always will be an unknown. Even those things God has chosen to share with us are veiled in mystery. He reveals the future one day, one hour, one minute at a time. While this may frustrate you at times, you would probably admit that given the opportunity to see your lives unfold before your eyes, you almost certainly would regret it.

It's true—you won't ever know what troubles might be scattered along the path ahead. What you can know is that God is always watching over you, listening for you, ready to help the moment you call. With his help, you can navigate whatever you may encounter.

∞

God, we thank you for lighting our path as we walk together through life. We will face each day with your help. Amen.

*Good people can look forward
to a bright future.*

Proverbs 13:9 NCV

Hiding Yourselves in Him

The LORD is good, a stronghold on a day of trouble; he protects those who take refuge in him.

Nahum 1:7 NRSV

Imagine for a moment that you walk out onto your porch and see a tornado barreling toward you. Thinking quickly, you grab your loved ones and possibly even your dog or cat and climb down into your storm shelter. Below ground in this safe place, you can hear the storm raging above you, but you are untouched by its fury.

In the Bible, God often compares himself to a cleft in the rock, a fortress, a sturdy hiding place, or a refuge. He is, for those who run to him, a shelter in the face of the storm. Why face your storms alone? Run to him. He is always there when you need him.

God, we are comforted to know that we can hide ourselves in you when the storms of life threaten to overtake us. Amen.

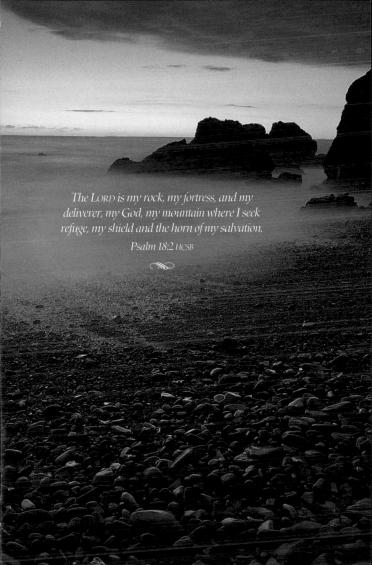

The LORD is my rock, my fortress, and my
deliverer, my God, my mountain where I seek
refuge, my shield and the horn of my salvation.

Psalm 18:2 HCSB

The Bible Sustains You

Anxiety weighs down the human heart, but a good word cheers it up.

Proverbs 12:25 NRSV

∞

The Bible is often referred to as God's Word because it is his communication, his message to humankind. The Bible is filled with wisdom and understanding, and reading it strengthens and sustains you spiritually, just as food strengthens and sustains you physically.

If you are anxious, you will find his invitation to bring your worries to him and receive his peace. If you are fearful, he invites you to hide yourselves in him. If you are lonely and troubled, he promises to stay with you to help you work things out. If you are hurt, he offers comfort. If you are confused, he gives clarity of mind. Go to the Bible, read his promises, and let his words feed your souls.

∞

God, we thank you for your Word, the Bible, and for all the many promises it contains, promises that strengthen and sustain us. Amen.

Jesus answered, "The Scriptures say: 'No one can live only on food. People need every word that God has spoken.'"

Matthew 4:4 CEV

Your Burden Bearer

*Blessed be the Lord,
who daily bears us up;
God is our salvation.*

Psalm 68:19 NRSV

∞

When you married, you each gained something significant and wonderful. You gained a partner with whom you can share life's burdens. No longer did you have to carry the weight of your troubles and responsibilities alone. You will find, though, that life sometimes dishes out more than even two people can handle. That's when God promises to come alongside and lift the weight from your shoulders. That's when he becomes your burden bearer.

Life is easier for some than for others, but each person has some load to bear. No matter what struggles the two of you face, God is there to help you by offering his shoulder to the load. And when he is lifting with you, your burdens become light.

~

God, when our burdens become too much for us to carry, we look to you. We are comforted to know you are always there to help. Amen.

Come to Me, all of you who are weary and
burdened, and I will give you rest.

Matthew 11:28 HCSB

He Is Your Strength

My body and mind may fail, but you are my strength and my choice forever.

Psalm 73:26 CEV

Have you ever suffered a loss or disappointment and had someone say, "Don't worry. You'll be stronger for it"? Did the experience leave you feeling stronger? Probably it left you feeling just the opposite. When the circumstances of life have beaten you up, you don't feel strong. You feel small, weak, and compromised.

God is the key to finding strength in your trials and tribulations, and the strength you find is not your own but his. When your body is exhausted and you are emotionally drained, reach out to the One who has what you need. Ask him to add his strength to your weakness and get you back in the game. You'll be stronger for it—guaranteed.

God, as we recognize what we are made of, we also recognize our need for you. Thank you for being there when we call. Amen.

Those who trust in the LORD will
renew their strength.

Isaiah 40:31 HCSB

No Fear

Those who are righteous will be long remembered. They do not fear bad news; they confidently trust the LORD to care for them.

Psalm 112:6–7 NLT

∞

Dwindling IRAs, increasing unemployment, wars, poverty, and disease. Watching the news can make you feel like crawling under the covers and refusing to come out. The trouble is, hiding from your fears won't make them disappear.

When the two of you feel overwhelmed by the realities around you, do something productive with your fear—give it away. God will exchange your fear for his peace and joy in every circumstance.

No one knows what will happen in the next hour let alone tomorrow, but God knows everything. He's aware of every dive in the stock market and every global conflict before it happens, and he has worked it all into his plan. Trust him and fear not.

God, we desire the security and confidence that comes from knowing you are walking with us. We will look up, and we will not fear. Amen.

I, the LORD your God,
will hold your right
hand, saying to you,
"Fear not, I will
help you."

Isaiah 41:13 NKJV

A Helping Hand

By helping each other with your troubles, you truly obey the law of Christ.

Galatians 6:2 NCV

A rewarding way to thank God for helping you through your tough times is by letting him use you to help someone else through a tough time. God may choose to whisper encouraging words to a person's heart or flood his or her mind and heart with peace. But when tangible, quantifiable help is needed, he uses people who are willing to step forward and lend a hand.

The two of you could be used of God to bring hope and help to someone who is hurting. All you need is compassion and a listening ear. He'll make who, what, when, and where clear to you. Such actions please God, bless others, and add joy and satisfaction to your lives.

We thank you, God, for the privilege of being used by you to help others. Your goodness brings us great joy. Amen.

Don't forget to help others and to share your possessions with them. This too is like offering a sacrifice that pleases God.

Hebrews 13:16 CEV

Eternal Rewards

Our light and momentary troubles are achieving for us an eternal glory that far outweighs them all.

2 Corinthians 4:17 NIV

Some would say that this life is a schoolhouse for eternity. It is where we learn our lessons, develop character, and build inner strength. The Bible doesn't confirm or deny that premise, but it does promise that God will use every circumstance we face in life to make us better people. It also promises that God will reward us each time we stand up, take hold of our faith, and overcome the trials and tribulations that assail us.

You might be thinking that God's love and comfort are quite enough reward for your hard times. Nevertheless, God sees fit to do more. He looks for excuses to bless his children.

God, you help us through the difficult places in life and then reward us as if we had done it all ourselves! How generous you are to us. Amen.

Be sure not to lose what we have worked for. If you do, you won't be given your full reward.

2 John 8 CEV

Never Give Up

God will strengthen you with his own great power so that you will not give up when troubles come, but you will be patient.

Colossians 1:11 NCV

∞

Dealing with difficult situations, financial hardships, medical problems, and relationship issues can be exhausting. Wanting to just give up and walk away is a human response, but giving up does not bring relief. Instead, it makes circumstances worse.

It's always best to face your troubles squarely, to deal with them, rather than sweep them under the carpet. That takes patience and courage, both of which may be in short supply. Even then, though, you have an option. Reach out to God. He will give you the strength you need to take charge of your circumstances and find real relief. When troubles come, don't give up; team up with God.

∞

God, we turn our eyes to you for the strength we need to face the adverse circumstances in our lives. Amen.

Don't quit in hard times. Pray all the harder.

Romans 12:12 MSG

He Has Overcome

[Jesus said] "In this world you will have trouble. But take heart! I have overcome the world."

John 16:33 NIV

Have you ever been in the midst of a difficult circumstance, feeling lost and confused, when a friend revealed to you that he or she had experienced that same circumstance with a positive outcome? That's always encouraging, isn't it? When you are going through something, especially for the first time, it's good to know that there really is nothing new under the sun. Your trials and tribulations look just like the ones that other people suffer.

God takes this one step further. Not only is he aware of every adverse circumstances that could possibly befall you, but he has also overcome each one, conquered it, and stripped it of its power. Take your troubles to God, and let him encourage your heart.

God, we thank you for your assurance that you have conquered and will help us conquer every adverse circumstance of life. Amen.

Since He Himself was tested and has suffered,
He is able to help those who are tested.

Hebrews 2:18 HCSB

Service

Keep in mind always that the ultimate
Master you're serving is Christ.

Colossians 3:24 MSG

First Serve God

Back when monarchies were the rule rather than the exception, one of the most coveted jobs any man or woman could have was to serve the king. Those positions were given exclusively to the best and brightest in the realm. The idea of "service" back then was considered a noble calling.

The Bible calls Jesus the King of all kings and God's Son. He has earned this distinction because of the service he rendered to humankind when he left his throne to be born as a human to reconcile us to our heavenly Father. Now this mighty King has invited you to serve him, enter his inner circle, and become part of his family. What could be grander?

God, we gladly serve King Jesus. Help us as we determine together to serve him with excellence and with joy. Amen.

The LORD Most High is awe-inspiring,
a great King over all the earth.

Psalm 47:2 HCSB

Using Your Gifts

Like good stewards of the manifold grace of God, serve one another with whatever gift each of you has received.

1 Peter 4:10 NRSV

Living in service to the King of kings has a simple and practical application here on earth. You serve both God the Father and God the Son by serving others. And each of you has been given certain gifts with which to do that.

It would make no sense for everyone to do the same thing, so these gifts vary widely. Some people have gifts of imparting wisdom and understanding; others have the gift of encouragement. Some have the ability to make soul-inspiring music through song or instrument. Still others have organizational, writing, or artistic gifts. There are as many gifts as there are people. Are the two of you aware of the gifts that reside in you for service to God?

God, we thank you for the gifts you have placed in us. Help us as we use them to serve you by serving others. Amen.

*Every good and perfect gift comes down from the
Father who created all the lights in the heavens.*

James 1:17 CEV

Serving God by Serving Others

*Keep your head in all
situations, endure hard-
ship, do the work
of an evangelist,
discharge all the duties
of your ministry.*
2 Timothy 4:5 NIV

∞

In the Bible, there are many accounts of Jesus' ministering to the needs of the crowds that followed him. He prayed for them, healed them, fed them, freed them from their fears, taught them how to be reconciled to God, and gave them hope for the future. Those who enter God's service carry on that work. People still need prayer, food, comfort, and hope. They need someone to inspire them. They need someone to help them.

Ask God how you can use your gifts in service to him. Then look around you. The opportunities are everywhere, and one of them will be a natural fit for the two of you.

Dear God, we thank you for the opportunity
to serve you by serving others. Show us where
our particular gifts can best be used. Amen.

The King will answer them, "I assure you: Whatever you did for one of the least of these brothers of Mine, you did for Me."

Matthew 25:40 HCSB

With All Your Heart

Serve wholeheartedly, as if you were serving the Lord, not men, because you know that the Lord will reward everyone for whatever good he does.

Ephesians 6:7–8 NIV

Serving humankind on God's behalf is a glorious pursuit but by no means an easy job. Someone will always refuse your service, arrogantly disregard it, or fault you for trying. At times you will be misunderstood, your motives will be challenged, and your good intentions will be cast aside.

When your service is spurned, you must remember that you are answering a higher calling. You are in service to God, and he alone will judge the quality and effectiveness of those actions you carry out on his behalf. He alone will reward you for the work you have done. As the two of you reach out to others, keep it in your hearts to please him.

God, show us how to serve others with the gifts you have given us. Open doors of service, we pray. Amen.

*Whatever you do, do it enthusiastically, as
something done for the Lord and not for men.*

Colossians 3:23 HCSB

In Your Own Way

There are different ways to serve the same Lord.

1 Corinthians 12:5 CEV

Since God has given a variety of gifts with which to serve others on his behalf, it is inevitable that some gifts will garner more attention than others will. For example, if you have been gifted with an extraordinary singing voice, you almost certainly will receive more praise and appreciation from others than someone whose gift is caring for the homeless.

What you must remember is that your attentiveness and faithfulness to the gift you have been given is of great value to God. Though it may go virtually unnoticed by others, he sees and highly esteems everything you do. As the two of you use the gifts you have been given, remember that you are serving God.

God, remind us often that there are no small gifts. Every gift you give has potential to bless you and others. Amen.

Do not neglect your gift.

1 Timothy 4:14 NIV

Signing Your Service

*Whatever your hand
finds to do, do with
your might.*

Ecclesiastes 9:10 NRSV

∞

Those who have been serving God for a long time would tell you they are sometimes tempted to give a little less than their best. Stress, fatigue, and so many other things can influence the quality of a person's service. They might tell you that they feel all their hard work is making little difference in the world or that those they are serving seem to have no understanding of the sacrifices being made on their behalf.

These same people would also tell you that one strategy for overcoming service overload is to mentally sign each act of service with your name and offer it to God as your best work. Remembering that you're doing it for him puts everything in perspective.

∽

God, help us never to take our gifts for granted,
but always let us strive for excellence in
our service to you. Amen.

*Whatever you do, in word or deed, do every-
thing in the name of the Lord Jesus, giving
thanks to God the Father through him.*

Colossians 3:17 NRSV

Strength to Serve

Whoever serves must do so with the strength that God supplies, so that God may be glorified in all things through Jesus Christ.

1 Peter 4:11 NRSV

The need is great. Hurting people are everywhere. Millions of hurting people are reaching for a hand up. The work can seem endless and overwhelming. It can consume everything you have, even to the neglect of your own needs and the needs of your loved ones.

When the two of you determine to serve God, you become part of his outstretched hand, his answer to those who cry out to him. God is pleased, but it is not God's desire for you to lose yourselves in the process. Be wise as you serve. Ask God to help you make good choices and strengthen you for the work at hand.

God, we need your wisdom and your strength as we step forward in your service. Thank you for giving us all we need. Amen.

*Wisdom is a tree of life to
those who embrace her.*

Proverbs 3:18 NLT

∞

Freedom to Serve

We have freedom now, because Christ made us free. So stand strong.
Galatians 5:1 NCV

∞

You know that your gifts have come from God, and you know that he intends for you to use them to bless and serve others. At the same time, serving God is a privilege rather than a requirement. Ulti-mately, it is yours to decide what, if anything, you will do with the gifts you have been given.

You would not be the first to ignore the gifts within you or fail to use them in the ways your Creator intended. God wants you to serve him freely. He will not coerce or intimidate you. He never bullies. He simply invites you to become all you were created to be and use your gifts to make a difference.

God, we joyfully accept your invitation to serve you by serving others. Thank you for the privilege. Amen.

If the Son makes you free,
you shall be free indeed.

John 8:36 NKJV

All You Have

Love GOD, your God, walk in all his ways, do what he's commanded, embrace him, serve him with everything you are and have.

Joshua 22:5 MSG

Serving God is a high calling. It is the best possible life. Serving God is an investment that will continue to resonate in eternity. And absolutely nothing the two of you do in pursuit of God's service will be wasted or forgotten. But walking it out is challenging. It is possible that you will face adversity and hardship and you that will be asked to make hard choices and bitter sacrifices.

Know this: If you give all you have, you will receive more than you could imagine in return. Do things God's way, and you will find that the more you give, the more you have left. Rejoice as you serve, and God will rejoice with you.

God, as we serve you, we know that you will be looking out for us. Thank you for all you do for us. Amen.

If you give to others, you will be given a full amount in return.

Luke 6:38 CEV

Whatever It Takes

I want you to do whatever will help you serve the Lord best, with as few distractions as possible.

1 Corinthians 7:35 NLT

Once you both have made the choice to serve God, your decision will be challenged repeatedly. There will be those who will tell you you're making a mistake, that serving God is a waste of your time and potential. You may encounter financial setbacks, health issues, and a vast array of other distractions.

When these things happen, hang on to your resolve. See these circumstances as your entrance exam, a test of your inner determination and mettle. You are about to begin the adventure of a lifetime, so begin by talking to God and trusting him to help you. If he is worthy of your service, he is worthy of your trust.

We look to you, God, for all our needs. We trust you to keep us determined and enthusiastic about serving you. Amen.

*Forgetting what is behind and reaching forward
to what is ahead, I pursue as my goal the prize
promised by God's heavenly call in Christ Jesus.*

Philippians 3:13–14 HCSB

The Best Reward of All

God is not unjust; he will not overlook your work and the love that you showed for his sake in serving the saints, as you still do.

Hebrews 6:10 NRSV

Those who have spent their lives serving God by serving others would almost certainly tell you that their work is its own reward. They draw great strength, satisfaction, and enjoyment from using their gifts to make a difference in people's lives. This includes missionaries who must live in dreadful conditions, those who have given up high-paying careers, and those who risk injury, disease, even death to do what they feel God has called them to do.

In addition, God says that he notices every good thing that is done in his name. He knows and is moved by it. Your service pleases him, and knowing that is the greatest reward of all.

God, we thank you for the joy that comes from serving you. Knowing you are pleased with us means everything. Amen.

*May the L*ORD *reward you for what you have done, and may you receive a full reward from the L*ORD *God.*

Ruth 2:12 HCSB

How amazing are the deeds of the LORD! All who delight in him should ponder them. Everything he does reveals his glory and majesty. His righteousness never fails.

Psalm 111:2–3 NLT

I will sing of the tender mercies of the LORD's unfailing love forever! Young and old will hear of your faithfulness. Your unfailing love will last forever.

Psalm 89:1–2 NLT